Dying to Live

Surviving Near-Death

A Self-Help Memoir by

CATHY GABRIELSEN

ISBN: 978-1-73439-623-2 (print)
ISBN: 978-1-73439-622-5 (ebook)

CONTENTS

DEDICATION

To my husband, my love, Scott,
for your constant and unwavering support—
but mostly for holding me tenderly while I healed
and for loving me unconditionally through it all.

FOREWORD
By Deborah King

Cathy Gabrielsen died twice—as a teenager in a horrific automobile accident in 1988, and again as a young mother of two small children in 2010—
only to be returned to life after an encounter with a miraculous healing
Light on the "other side." Crossing the boundary into death, she experienced a spiritual transformation, the release of pain and fear, while discovering her own hidden paranormal gifts—and now shares her full story in
Dying To Live: Surviving Near-Death.

Cathy's heart-stopping journey—from surviving a near-fatal car crash
to battling a breast cancer diagnosis and sepsis to battles with depression,
anxiety and PTSD—explodes with untamed honesty. How does facing
death change us? What is it like to die? The answer in these pages will star-
tle you, illuminate you, inspire you. You may read a thousand books on
facing death; Cathy will show you how to face life.

Never has there been a truer, more transcendent depiction of near-
death than in the life of Cathy Gabrielsen.

Dying to Live

PROLOGUE
The After Life

THE COUNTRY ROAD STRETCHES AHEAD, TWISTING AND winding toward Pennsylvania Route 113. In the moonlight the two-lane asphalt glimmers. The few icebox houses we've passed are deserted, and the November stars shine high in the sky, for it is nearly midnight.

A single car, a 1987 Ford Bronco, lies at the bottom of a ravine on this road, flipped on its side, windshield shattered, roof smashed.

Slumped behind the Bronco's wheel, moaning in pain in the wreckage, is my boyfriend Tom. The steering wheel has crushed Tom's lung, and is rammed against his chest, stopping the oxygen to his brain. He drifts in and out of consciousness.

I'm in the passenger seat. Broken glass, mud and blood trickle in sheets down my face. It's the 11th of November, 1988, and I am 18 years old.

"Cathy?" Tom murmurs, gazing dizzily around. "Is Cathy OK?" He closes his eyes, his throat gurgling unintelligible words. "Help, we need help," he groans, raising his head to look at me. Then Tom buries his face against the wheel and falls silent.

Please God, my thoughts whisper. *Help us. How did this happen? How did we get here?*

Minutes before, we'd been driving to a high school party in nearby Chester Springs. Upon arrival, Tom and I were turned away at the door. Seeing my disappointment, Tom gently grabbed my hand.

"Let's go," he said, nodding back toward his Bronco. "We'll find the next party."

As we drove off, Tom stared into the rearview mirror, certain he saw a police officer approaching the party house we'd just left. This made him panic, pushing the Bronco to full-throttle.

Veering onto two-lane Kimberton Road, at the intersection to Route 113, he missed the turn, steering straight into a farmer's pasture, not seeing that ahead of us lay a 15-foot drop.

The car plummeted, nose-first, crashing into the ground at high speed, plunging to the bottom of a muddy ravine.

For what seemed like an eternity we sat trapped there. Now blinking my eyes, I feel blood dribble from my hairline. I struggle, unable to move, wedged into my seat by the locked safety belt.

We wait. Five minutes. Ten. I talk to Tom, begging to hear his voice, but he doesn't answer. The car is a jumble of mud and shattered glass. Closing my eyes, I try to shut this vision out, to shut everything out, letting my mind drift.

A flash of fear hits me. Suddenly I don't feel any pain. I don't feel my arms, my legs. I don't feel anything.

As I sink into unconsciousness, I experience a powerful force pulling me from Tom's car. *What is this?* As I gaze up, an opening, a dark space appears. My body is propelled into darkness, down a channel, a tunnel, moving at high speed. As the channel widens I'm embraced by a peaceful, blinding white light. The light is filled with love. The light is repairing my wounds, healing my heart. I hear music—magnificent music, the most beautiful music emanating from all around me, pouring into me like the piercing love of the light.

The light hugs me, comforts me, holds me as I move with it, higher and higher. It feels like home. I float in the love and comfort and arms of the light. A sense of warmth and peace engulfs me.

Please God, let me stay here.

I listen, hearing a tranquil voice in my head. "My daughter Cathleen, it is not your time. There is too much work to be done." There's no judgment in the voice, only pure love. I surrender to the voice, and the light claims me, as I slip into its radiant arms.

At that moment I hear a grinding, mechanical shriek. The light fades. It becomes a pinprick, a tiny speck in the distance. The channel widens. I'm being drawn by unseen hands back toward the end of the tunnel.

Can I choose to go back? No. The tunnel widens. I'm traveling at greater and greater speed. I wake to loud voices, to hands jerking me out of the passenger seat, lifting me out of the vehicle, placing me in an ambulance. I hear rescue teams scurrying around, urgently trying to remove Tom from the Bronco, their voices frightened, hopeless. I want to reach out, to hug Tom, hold his hand, tell him everything's going to be okay. In a panic I'm screaming and crying for the medics to let me go.

The hands of the medics gently stroke my head. Their voices whisper to me. *I have come back,* I realize. I've reawakened, and I've survived death— my first death. I am no longer in the light.

I'm alive.

Looking back on that November night, I recall the terror I'd felt, waiting for rescue. Yet in that moment of near-death, my "lifeless" body radiated life, as the "Light" (as I later referred to it) cradled and carried me, revealing a bold new future to me. *You don't have to die,* it whispered, *to be connected to the Light. You can live free of fear, connected in service to the Light, to all that is.*

The Light showed me the power of redemption and forgiveness. The Light revealed my purpose. The Light offered me a vision of what my life almost was, and what it still could be. My first near-death experience was the first step toward a second chance, a rebirth, a new life.

This book is my story. This is my truth, my testament, my reawakening. This is my transformation.

This is my *after* life.

PART ONE

THE CROSSROADS

How sharp the knife is
That slices the skin.
Sharper is the pain that lies
Within.

1

My Accident and First Near-Death

THE NEXT MORNING, I WOKE IN INTENSIVE CARE, IN A LOCAL hospital. I lay in bed, wracked by pain, slipping in and out of nightmares, floating in and out of consciousness. In my lucid moments, I queried the nurses, wondering what had happened to Tom. Later I learned Tom had been flown to the Hospital of the University of Pennsylvania, fifty miles away, where he was in critical care.

Miraculously, my injuries were neither severe nor life-threatening: a concussion, 150 stitches in my face, and a bruised heart. *How is that possible?* I wondered. As I waited to hear further news about Tom, and the hospital refused to answer my questions, a panic washed over me. *What is everyone hiding?*

A week later, after being discharged, I received a phone call from Tom's brother-in-law. Tom was in a coma. He'd suffered a traumatic brain injury. Beginning at the scene of the accident and after admittance to the hospital, he'd died 9 times that night, each time being resuscitated back to life. The lack of oxygen had caused an immense amount of pressure to build in his brain. As his brain swelled, permanent neurological damage resulted. The odds were he would never awaken.

As I hung up, shock vibrated through me. My mind was unable to process the news; it felt as if something inside of me cracked, and I was unable to breathe. I had no idea what a coma was, other than what I'd seen on TV, where the characters seemed to blink their eyes and awaken in what seemed to be a magical moment.

As I rushed to the hospital, an iron-clad resolution built in me. *Perhaps they'll use a wonder drug on Tom,* I concluded, refusing to surrender hope. Approaching the Critical Care ward, down a white corridor that seemed to stretch forever, I was met at the doors by Tom's mother. A stoic look of calm covered this petite woman's face.

"Cathy," she said, gripping my hand, "life can be hard and challenging. This is one of those times." I nodded. As our eyes met, suddenly her face became more serious. "Never let life or its difficulties make you bitter, or change you in any way."

Though I would carry these words with me for the rest of my life, at that moment I wondered what she meant. I expected my voice, my presence would awaken Tom. Then the doors swung back. Walking down the long corridor with Tom at the end, I was ushered into a new world, a world flipped upside-down, a world where grief and death loomed over everything.

Where my life would never be the same.

Standing at the foot of Tom's bed, I couldn't believe what I was seeing.

Tom had been a surfer, a wrestler, muscular and fierce, full of fire and passion. Now he lay in intensive care, in a coma, surrounded by machines—so many machines that there wasn't room for visitors. Monitors beeped his erratic heartbeat. Life-support machinery gurgled and swished. Tubes fed into his body from everywhere, a bag collecting his urine. The tube embedded in his throat seemed so painful that it took my breath away.

I stared frozen, in disbelief, shocked to see Tom so fragile, so incapacitated. I didn't recognize the Tom I'd once known, the free spirit who loved the ocean, the wrestler who listened to the Grateful Dead and Ziggy Marley. Only yesterday we'd dared to dream of going off to college together—Tom to Roanoke in Virginia, me to Mount St. Mary's in Maryland.

One moment, he was a beautiful boy with teenage hopes and dreams—the next, he was a coma patient hooked up to machines and struggling to survive.

My mind grappled to understand, grasping for words of comfort, wanting to say, *I'm here, Tom. I am here with you.* The whoosh of the respirator reverberated over the pounding of blood in my ears. Yet I couldn't stop looking at him. I felt the need to hold Tom's hand, to touch his head, to sing to him, to talk to him. I wouldn't allow myself to believe he wasn't going to be healed, that Tom wasn't going to make it. As long as I believed my prayers would be answered, I had hope.

Anything less was never an option.

Tom stayed at the University of Pennsylvania Hospital a few months. When the doctors could do no more, he was moved to a rehabilitation facility, then to a nursing home, and finally back to his family home. The plan was simple: Tom would heal and get well. Then we'd go off to college and get on with our lives, and this nightmare would be over.

I sat with him, day in and day out. He couldn't talk, eat, drink or control any body movement. My visits were an opportunity for Tom's mom to take a much-needed break. I swabbed his mouth when it looked dry. I stroked his forehead, and repositioned his hands. I showed him photographs, to remind him of his past. I composed notes to Tom's mom, at the end of each visit, telling her of the day's events. *Tom looked good today,* I'd write. *He blinked his eyes. I think I saw a smile on his face. The Cat Stevens music I played seemed to calm him.* I'd tell her if the tube feeding went easily, if his eyes followed me around the room, who came to visit, and how Tom responded. I tried to fill each note with optimism, with positivity. With hope.

I'd tell her these things and more, to ease her aching heart. I dedicated my life to Tom, to faith and prayer, living in the hope that Tom would heal. That he'd rise out of his hospital bed, and walk again.

Tom's awakening from the coma was gradual. Over time, his eyes opened, and he was able to blink them, in answer to my questions, multiple times for *Yes* and once for *No.* Yet there never was that Hallmark Channel moment of revival, of magical, teary-eyed reunion. There was only the heartwrenching process of racing to his bed when his eyelids fluttered or his hands moved an inch, and the always-devastating blow to hear the doctors say, "It was a reflex. We may not see more."

These were the loneliest days. I mourned the life Tom would never have. I mourned those who would never meet the Tom I'd known, never benefit from his boyish smile, his laugh. I mourned to think he'd never again surf the ocean waves, riding a surfboard on two strong legs, so wild, so free. Finally, I mourned the life I had lost. Everyone I knew was living their best life, while I was living Tom's slow, tortured descent.

As Tom's life flattened out, without goals, without a future, my life slowly faded away. As the years blurred together, all my plans changed. Instead of leaving for college I remained at home, commuting to a local university. I attended classes at night, visiting Tom during each day, struggling to find balance in my life, until I was failing every course.

All sense of myself evaporated. I'd become a spectator, disconnected from the world outside, watching a boy who could breathe and blink, whose eyes showed pain, anger and confusion, who made a sound like a laugh when he was told a joke—a boy just trying to be, to do *something*—while I waited for somebody somewhere someday to show me how to move on.

How to let go.

How to forgive myself for surviving.

How to *live*.

Desperately I longed for a happy ending to the story. Never did it occur to me that nursing and caring for Tom might become my own private prison.

Years ticked by. Tom went on living like this. Day after day, I returned to his bedside, coaxing him into his wheelchair, feeding Tom his meals. He looked at me, his piercing blue eyes alert, those blue eyes seeming to say to me, *I'm still here.*

Our relationship remained constant. Somehow I managed to blend my two lives: my life caring for Tom, and my life outside Tom. Rarely did I think about my own brush with death, or the tunnel of Light I'd experienced; it was all too puzzling. Unable to let go of the guilt I felt for surviving—and the greater guilt I'd feel from hurting Tom and his mother, should I choose to walk away to live my own life—I harbored the unbearable weight of self-blame in my heart. Self-hatred crushed the life out of me. If I hurt, if I suffered, that felt reasonable: I deserved it. I could live with the hurt.

Six years had now passed. Six years after the accident, I was wallowing in guilt and self-punishment. I began to wean my visits. I stopped visiting Tom every day, instead coming just a few times a week. Then less. And less.

Still, I remained a presence in Tom's life. I would drive his family's handicapped van with Tom in his wheelchair, fastened into place—sometimes to an old friend's home, or his school homecoming game. I attended parties with Tom, and he visited my home. Later he would sit in the front row at my wedding. And I would go on to speak the eulogy at his funeral.

Little did I know that the night of the accident—the two of us trapped inside the wreckage of his car—would be the last time I heard Tom's gentle voice. His last words—"Is Cathy okay?"— would continue to haunt me, replaying in an endless loop in my brain. Everything that happened that night was rewinding in my head like an out-of-order movie, fractions of a second flashing here and there, as if a longer glimpse of the Light I'd seen might blind me forever.

2

Safest in Silence

IN THE YEARS FOLLOWING THE ACCIDENT, AND MY BRUSH with near-death, fear continued to stalk me.

I was crippled by fear: Fear of loss, fear of death, fear of cars. Riding in a car meant the possibility of a crash. Strapped in the passenger seat, I'd replay the accident over and over in my mind, scanning the oncoming traffic, fingers clutched tight to the door handle. Seeing brake lights, I'd immediately fear a collision, and cry out, "Red lights, *red lights!*" Over time, I preferred to be the driver; it felt easier—and safer—to be the driver.

Over time, the terror of cars would get the better of me.

At the encouragement of my mother, I found myself at a therapist's office. The therapist's advice stunned me. "I don't think you realize," she explained, "that you have the right to be happy. To live a life free of fear." Yet I was too damaged, broken into pieces of myself, still controlled by a sense of unworthiness, so her words fell on deaf ears. I was not worthy of living a happy, fulfilling life.

People say happiness is a choice. Yes, I yearned to be happy; I just didn't know *how*. Instead, my life slowed to a standstill. It seemed impossible to go on living as if Tom were fully healed, as if he'd walked away from the accident, as if his free spirit had returned to wrestling and surfing after that night, as if nothing had happened.

I should be grateful, I told myself, *because I survived.* Unfortunately, surviving for me would only have been a gift if we'd both actually survived. Tom's life to me—unable to walk, to talk, to drive his beloved Bronco, to feed himself—was not surviving.

You are the person who should be in that wheelchair, my mind repeated, *not Tom. You should have done something different that night.* I coped by trying to make it up to his family, his friends, to the rescuers and doctors and everyone involved—unable to admit the lie I'd fabricated, that during the accident I'd asked Tom if he was okay, as if that would have changed what had happened to him.

Ultimately, I coped by depriving myself of joy. I buried myself under tremendous guilt. Each time I felt strong and resolved to let it go, I recalled my near-death experience. Each time, rather than propelling myself forward, I was hurled backward again into that abyss.

Silently I waited for things to change. While I waited, I surrendered my power and self-worth to others, to anyone who needed me. I waited for the people who loved me and cared for me to say, "You have done enough." I waited for somebody to tell me I could stop sacrificing every moment of every day for everyone else. I waited for somebody to say they would still love me, if I decided to move on, and take care of me.

I waited.

And waited.

Years passed.

But no one ever told me "enough."

I don't recall if I stopped talking to people, or if people stopped talking to me.

The thought of being around people made me tremble; being with people meant I needed to converse with them, to open myself, to *talk*. The conversations always revolved around *me*: I was the girl in the car accident. The girl with the disabled boyfriend. The girl who'd survived a near-death experience—an NDE, I'd later learn these episodes in the Light were called.

I was a downer. I knew it. So I avoided people, and conversations.

I felt safest in silence. I felt safest in prayer. The last thing I wanted to talk about was my NDE, my encounter with death, the tunnel, the voice I heard or the Light. People might think I was crazy.

I felt safest *alone*. Eventually, I just stopped talking.

As the years passed, my voice remained silent. I would never speak of my NDE. *No one will understand.* The overwhelming consensus among my family and friends was something must be wrong with me. I was defective, broken, damaged beyond repair. I couldn't be "fixed," so I spent those years isolating myself, my future blunted as if by a sledge-hammer, stripped of any connection to the outside world.

Connection. That's what I longed for—for someone to feel me as I felt others. For someone to see my plight, my turmoil, my disengagement from a real life, and give me purpose, show me direction.

Exiled from others, I sought places to be alone, away from the judging eyes always surrounding me. These hidden places became my safe spots. Lone tables in libraries. Shadowy upstairs hallways. Unfamiliar restaurants, far from the college campus. I'd hunt out the lonely places no student would want to be. I'd find a place to get away from everyone, anyone, who might know me, or my situation, or want to talk.

From my safe spot, I could turn my mind away from my NDE, from the darkness of the black tunnel, and the panic of being unwillingly returned from the Light; instead, I'd try to find some Light in my everyday. I'd watch other people laughing. I'd spy on their effortless life. I imagined them watching me, whispering about me, pointing at me, wondering about me. The second anyone caught my eye, I'd tuck my head back into my book, and keep it buried there, embarrassed to be alone. As they crossed the room to brush past me I held my breath, hoping and praying they wouldn't stop, that they'd pass me by, that they would come no closer.

My prayers were answered. They never did. Yet inside, I wept.

As the months and years ticked away, the circle of family and friends visiting Tom slowly ebbed.

Immediately after the accident, there'd been abundance of relatives, wrestling buddies, neighbors, support, tears, and connection. Everyone prayed together, stayed in the hospital room together, hoping for that miracle. Days would pass, then weeks, then months, then years. As the time passed, and no miracle arrived, one by one the people left. As they did, my heart was torn in two, until the day I found myself also disconnecting.

In the months to come, Tom's mother and I became the last ones remaining—I stuck with him, plugging and unplugging Tom's tubes, holding his hand, mopping his forehead, my mind creating imaginary responses to the conversations we'd never have. My life—which up to this point had been unraveling—was now in tatters. My response to the others leaving was revelatory: I could understand the reasons they disappeared. They were unable to bear their own grief.

Detached from control of my own destiny—and still awakening soaked in sweat from flashbacks of what I'd experienced inside Tom's wrecked car—I sought desperately to heal myself by healing others. *I need to heal them, so that I can feel better. I need to heal them, so that I can heal myself.*

Healing others would become the way to forget my near-death. Healing would become my compulsion, my fixation, my obsession, my escape from the everyday pressures of living. Healing would become the only thing I sought.

But could I become a healer? What right did I have to think that, to believe that? Recalling my near-death, being drawn through the darkness and into the loving Light, gave me a powerful, romantic sense of my destiny. *Healing must be the reason I still exist,* I reasoned. *Healing is what gives me value.*

Yet my brain still hammered out a different message: This was all a lie. As I struggled with confidence, with low self-esteem, I lost my will. I lost hope. Deep within me, I'd always believed I could heal Tom. My hands on him, my prayers over him, my time with him—these efforts of mine would make him better. They never did. I failed at healing. I failed at helping him. I let Tom down.

More appallingly, I'd let down Mary, the Virgin Mary—the Holy Mother, the Divine Feminine in my life. Mary, who had always stood with me, helped me through troubled times, always been there for me, always healed my agonies.

At the age of 5, I was chosen to be Mary, in the school Christmas show. I was also selected to be Mary for the May Processions at our Catholic academy, to wear the white dress and flowing veil that every girl dreamed of wearing. When I walked in those processions as Mary, my imagination took over and became my reality—I believed Mary was with me, walking in me as I held the bouquet of flowers, placing them at the foot of Mary's statue. I imagined she and I were one.

Mary was my other mother, my sweet, merciful mother; I could talk to her without fear as a child, tell her my truths as a teen, and beg for her mercy as an adult. I was told she loved me unconditionally, and she would always be there for me.

Yet now I'd let Mary down. And because I'd let Mary down, pulling away from my faith was now safer. If I didn't think of Mary, I wouldn't feel her disappointment. Deadened, I turned my spiritual Light off and stopped seeking. My faith was smashed.

In the aftermath, I began craving a deeper isolation. I needed solitude without judgment. I found that solitude in writing poetry.

Poetry became my private devotion, my therapy. Poetry became my safe place. Poetry became a way to express some of the grief and pain about my accident, to release the accusations and self-scorn that came with surviving.

In writing, my body could let out its primal scream. In writing, I could be the master of my feelings. I could control the tidal wave of my turbulent emotions as I scribbled them out:

Yesterday

Each salty drop
stung
my face
as it glided downward.
Each drop contained a memory,
a hope or inspiration.
They fell
One by one
away from my sight.
The drops came down
Heavier, in greater amounts
Falling

from me.
Only yesterday…
I smiled.

3

Is Your Love Strong Enough?

"CATHY, ARE YOU *CRAZY?!* YOU CAN'T KEEP PASSING UP THESE opportunities!"

All my life, I'd longed to experience love—I'd spent my lifetime, giving love. Giving love was easy. My experience with love was only felt when I gave.

Seeing my dilemma, my girlfriends worked hard to help me find love. Each time I'd dream about the possibility of a life with someone able to love me—a life with a husband, a home, children and joy—I'd become buried under the guilt and shame of leaving my friend Tom behind.

What would people think? What would they say?

Their negative thoughts hurtled through my head. They shut me back down, telling me I would be terrible, I would be abominable if I moved on and married.

Close to Christmas one year, my sister and our friends met to celebrate at a restaurant. Hearing another girlfriend was down the street at a nearby bar, I hustled off to find her.

Walking into this smoky bar, I spied my girlfriend talking to a few guys. "Come with me, we're all down the street," I beckoned, grabbing her hand. As we walked away, leaving the guys looking puzzled, one of them asked, "Who's *she?*" and my girlfriend jokingly replied, "That's Cathy, and she's *hopeless!*"

She was right. I was. I had no hope for a future. All I could see was a dim vision of a future—one of which I was unworthy.

Returning to my sister and our friends at the restaurant, I was suddenly approached by one of the guys from the bar. He begged for my phone number; I wouldn't give it to him.

"If you really want it," I boldly said, "you'll find a way to get it."

My friends were shocked. "Are you *crazy?!*" they whispered. "This guy will think you're insane! He'll never call!"

I admit, I must've been crazy. Mystifying as it now seems, this gorgeous guy—Scott, I later found out—somehow tracked down my number. Every day for months, he'd call and ask, "Where are we going tonight for dinner?" Finally one day, I caved. As I sat eating alfredo at a quaint Italian restaurant in Philadelphia that night, I remember catching myself thinking, *I could marry this guy.*

It took months before I allowed myself to receive what Scott was offering. When I finally opened my heart to him I don't recall. We began dating; after a few months, both of us knew we were meant to be married.

Still, my heart struggled. It had become apparent after so many years that Tom would never recover—yet no one spoke those words. No one spoke the words that it would be okay if Cathy decided to have a relationship, or to become married. And I never spoke the words to them, that I craved a new life. Everyone assumed Tom and I would be the same couple we were in high school.

Yet now here I was. Secretly engaged, and about to be married—and unable to free myself from the grip of fear this secret held me in, the fear of telling Tom's mom the truth.

For days, I couldn't shake the panic I felt. I knew there would be damage. I knew hurt and sadness would be coming her way. *Is your love for Scott strong enough to handle this?* I wondered.

Finally it was time—our engagement announcement would run in the newspaper the next day. For hours I sat staring at my phone until I'd worked up enough courage to call. As I spoke the words, "I'm engaged, and getting married" my heart sped up—*What will she say?*—yet she reacted just the way I knew she would. She wanted only the best for me.

In that moment, amid my joy of being engaged, were flashes of shame and guilt, for acknowledging the unspoken words: That Tom would never be well again. I'm certain she cried that day for me and Tom. Once, our hearts had been united in hopeful solidarity; now they were united in untold grief.

The day of my wedding came. After walking down the aisle and standing beside Scott at the altar, Tom was escorted toward us in his wheelchair, and placed with my family in the front row. Scott accepted the relationship I'd had with Tom. I never resolved the issues within me, the issue of my guilt. I never had the conversation with myself, that it was okay to love someone else, that I wasn't a bad person for living a life I wanted.

At last, it was over. My secret was out. Still, I felt plagued with unworthiness. I was unworthy of a life filled with happiness and love, or a future. I would not allow myself that. All I'd allow was the shame and pain I'd caused Tom's family to leave me for this one day.

Just long enough to let go. Just enough to move on. It was time.

4

Hello, Cancer

IN THIS SEASON OF WONDERFUL POSSIBILITIES, THE DARK IN my heart continued to fester. The dark in my heart emerged stronger than ever, cloaking me in deeper self-loathing. The dark in my heart crushed my dreams. The dark in my heart choked the magic of everyday life as a new bride into depression. The dark in my heart strangled this season of new hopes, new possibilities, new freedoms.

The dark in my heart eventually led to breast cancer.

It was 2003. I was 32 years old now, married, with a baby and a toddler.

In a way, I wasn't surprised by the diagnosis. Cancer was my punishment. I'd done something wrong, so I must suffer. Part of me believed it was a result of the car accident, the result of being selfish, witnessing my own death and returning, then wanting a life better than the life I had, the life I'd been blessed with.

It was my curse for having survived. And I accepted the punishment.

At the time of my diagnosis, life was good. We were fortunate to live in a beautiful new home; I was happy to be a mom, driving a navy-blue Volvo wagon with two car seats by day, a religious studies teacher by night.

Then the news came down.

Part of me always knew I'd contract breast cancer. I can't explain why; hearing the news I was neither shocked nor surprised. For weeks, I'd been experiencing pain in my breast. I'd visit the doctor and be told it was a result of having the baby and breastfeeding, among other things. For awhile, I dismissed it.

One day, as I was in the kitchen washing and drying dishes while the children napped, I overheard an *Oprah* show segment on the importance of mammograms. *Better safe than sorry,* I thought, and scheduled another appointment with my doctor.

After my mammogram, the nurse asked me to wait in a separate room for the results. I had no idea if that was standard protocol; I'd never gone in for a mammogram. So I sat and waited, alone. Alarms sounded in my head, screaming at me to leave. Finally the doctor arrived. "We found something that doesn't look benign," he stated.

Not benign? I wondered. *What does that mean?* My body shook. Seeing my expression, he looked flustered, then stated the awful truth. "It looks like there may be cancer in your breast."

A wave of despair hit me. Clutching my brown envelope with the large scan of my breast I left. "This may be nothing," the doctor tried reassuring me, "but it looks like something. You need to see a breast surgeon."

When I finally made it home, I slammed the front door and leaned against it, struggling to slow my breath. Days later, I met my surgeon. "Fast Hands," I called him—he talked fast, his hands moved fast, everything was fast. Showing me the image of my mammogram, I could see there were spots everywhere on my breast.

"This can't be cancer," Fast Hands said, shaking his head. "You're too young, and this isn't displaying the way cancer does. I bet you have a 2% chance of having cancer."

In the comfort of his sterile white medical suite, I believed him. A follow-up biopsy was scheduled. Outside his office, I heaved a sigh of relief. My inner peace was broken by his next phone call, the Wednesday after my biopsy.

"First, I want to say that you are going to live a long and healthy life," he told me in a pained voice, then sighed. "But you have a breast carcinoma, a very early stage, and we need to discuss your options."

My options?

I was stunned. *There it is,* I thought. *The 2%.* I had cancer. And I was going to have a mastectomy.

My husband Scott was devastated. Yet Scott did what he always did— he let his emotions pass. Scott's crying at tender moments has always been one of his most endearing qualities. He cried, and then he became a super- hero, which was everything I needed him to be.

As the days wore on toward my mastectomy, my mind returned again and again to that 2%. That 2% haunted me. The cycle continued: Being wheeled into surgery, I learned there was a 2% chance the cancer had spread out of my milk ducts.

After surgery, tests showed that the cancer *had* spread. Again I was rattled by this bizarre connection to the 2%. *Why me?* I wondered, trying to steel myself for more bad news. It was an aggressive form of cancer; fortu- nately, it had been detected early, so I was given a good chance at survival.

After recovery, I couldn't wait for Scott to bring me home. The results of the tests were burned in my brain, ringing in my ears the first few days. Every mistake in my life now seemed rolled out as more evidence I was unworthy, undeserving of any stroke of good luck, any mercy.

Finally came the day when Scott and I saw I had no breast. We stood together in the bathroom, the white tile floor below our feet. He untied my robe and I watched the gauze pads flutter to the floor, keeping my head down, gazing at the bandages on the ground. It was only after I finally heard him whisper in my ear, "You are so beautiful," that I looked up. I had been his young, fit bride. Now I'd exposed my new self—a breastless woman, standing naked before the man who loved me so.

At that moment, we were both standing in the crossroads. We had reached an intersection in our lives—where the road would go from here, neither of us could say. In all the craziness that lay behind and ahead—from near-death experiences to cancer—we would walk the path beside each other, always together.

Almost.

I spent most of the next few days sleeping. I felt a surge of shame for bringing the cancer into my family. I didn't want to be a burden—I wanted to prove I was still capable, I was strong, able to care for myself. I wanted to be superwoman through my cancer, not a burden.

I returned to my safe place—to the solitude and isolation that gave me comfort. I chose to be alone again. Alone I wouldn't have to talk about what I was thinking or feeling. Alone I could handle doctor's appointments, more tests, more bad news.

I wanted to face this crisis, alone.

Again, I was in a place that no one could understand. Counselors and hospital nurses advised me to join groups, gatherings of other women battling breast cancer. No, I said, no. They'd never understand how I felt. How could they? These women weren't me. This cancer was mine to deal with, to fight and to overcome, on my own.

What I wanted was my breast back. I wanted the body I'd known. I wanted to be the wife and mom I'd been before cancer.

I'd wake every day, wracked by pain. All the tissue on my chest had been removed. I couldn't lay down, or get up—any movement, even walking, was excruciating.

Women experiencing a mastectomy are advised to carry a pillow—it goes under the arm, protecting the arm from further damaging the wounds of the chest. When I came home, my 3-year-old son would hide my pillow. He'd dart out of our bedroom, tucking it under the couch. He hated that pillow. That pillow represented my pain, and he didn't want to see me with it.

My son's loving actions cut through me like a knife. Through it all I remained stoic. I suffered in silence, never letting anyone see my pain. The loss, the pain, the fear, the grief, the worry, the sadness—all remained hidden deep within me for years. Eventually they made their way to the surface, in the form of anxiety, depression, and PTSD.

I could feel my children's pain, their concern for their mother. I felt them pulling closer, holding me tighter. They were afraid: Mom was different, mom was wounded. Crying in the shower one day, as the water fell unobstructed from my right side, it washed over the area that once was my breast. I cried, not for my lost breast, but because I could not cuddle my children any longer. Caressing them now, injured as I was, filled every cell in my body with burning pain.

Yet I continued doing everything—the cooking, the cleaning, the caring for our children. Overdoing became my cross, and I carried it, slung over one shoulder, while with the other hand I managed to do it all. I refused to allow myself to just be, to heal, to rest, to take care of myself when I was sick. I wanted no one taking care of me.

The overdoing cost me more surgeries. I would pull apart stitches to the drains, open the wound that should have been closed. I pushed myself, beyond what was normal. And I would go back, after each setback, and do it all again.

One day, feeling particularly tired, I took a nap. Taking a nap was a great risk: Everyone would know something was brewing, something was wrong with mom. Lying prone in bed, I was unable to get up. I'd been struck with a high fever, and immense pain.

To ease the pain, I stumbled to the kitchen, pouring myself some hot water with lemon, thinking I'd bring it to my room, lay in my bed, and allow another night to pass.

Leaving the kitchen, the cup slipped from my hands, crashing onto my foot. The boiling water wasted no time soaking deep into my sock.

Frantically I raced to pull the sock off, being scorched by the boiling water. As I did, with the sock came all of my skin. And there it was, my foot, burned as badly as my breast from dozens of radiation treatments.

Are you kidding me?! my mind shrieked. That night I made a frantic call to the doctor, who immediately prescribed anti-depressants. It was the beginning of my relationship with prescription drugs. A new way to cope, to soothe, to comfort. Another way to ease the pain.

Even journaling, even poetry—which so often had been my savior—failed to ease my pain. In my sickness, my sorrow, I composed these notes, to my cancer, to my broken body, to God, to anyone who would listen:

My breast soft
My breast supple
My breast tender
My breast real
My breast sensuous
My breast woman
My breast
Gone.

Yet during these dark days, during the times I had pulled away from Mother Mary, from my spirituality, even when I wasn't aware of it, I was never alone. The Light surrounded me.

Encircled by other cancer patients at the treatment center—each battling their own war against an ever-invasive disease—I felt their own Light. So many cancer patients with children, like me, would receive their treatment, then leave to begin the first of their *two* jobs, before heading home to care for their children. Inspired by them, I found myself slowly pulling my life together again.

Though I'd experienced radiation treatments, multiple surgeries and so many complications I'd lost count, I knew my road was easier than that of so many others. With cancer, there is no judgment. Everyone has a stage, a grade. Some, like breast cancer, can be embarrassing to talk about. I felt embarrassed about my cancer. People would tell me they were sorry, and I'd shrug it off, casually replying, "It's nothing, it's an early stage. I could be much worse, I'm fine."

What I should have said was, "Thank you." What I should have said was, "It sucks, *really* sucks to only have one breast." But saying it made me feel as if I were complaining. As if I were whining.

So I said nothing.

Instead I swallowed my thoughts, went home, sat in my basement, and played superheroes with my two little boys. Their imaginative play soothed me. Envisioning the brave fantasies other moms and dads would need to create, just to make it through their day, I saw the power in imagination, inventing one's own world, one's own destiny. Seeing this gnawing black hole in these parents' lives, I made a vow to help them fill it. And that changed everything.

To homes where there was cancer, I brought bins of toys, and boxes of games. I sat and played with the kids, telling mom and dad to go rest, to take a nap. I sat with babies who'd lost their mother to cancer, feeling the love of their mom come through me, as if she were holding them herself.

I was on a mission, to bring joy and happiness to people who needed it. After a year of providing this support myself, I founded a non-profit organization, Cuddle My Kids, and spent the next 10 years caring for families with cancer.

Being a support system for others gave me an identity: healer. During the quiet moments of the night when my own children were peacefully sleeping, I felt a transformation, that I'd turned my life around. Struggling day-to-day with living this new version of myself—a breast-less and scarred woman—I was helping other women in crisis to heal. I accepted this new challenge with gusto, oddly believing for the first time in my life that perhaps all things were possible. *Maybe I'll be okay,* I announced to myself. *Maybe I don't need to accept that my story will have a messy ending. Something new is coming.*

Something new is about to begin.

5

My Second Near-Death

IT WAS 2010. SEVEN YEARS AFTER MY BREAST SURGERY. TWO years earlier, Tom had died in his sleep, after suffering for 19 years. Days before his funeral, I'd been asked to speak his eulogy. My mind froze. I sat in bed, fear burning at the back of my throat. *What the hell am I supposed to say for your eulogy, Tom?* Suddenly words came flooding out; I heard Tom's gentle voice, unwavering as a flame, saying two words: *Thank you.* It was all gratitude, full of thank you's and blessings. It was the first time Tom had spoken to me in 19 years; wherever he was, however he was communicating, I knew he was no longer suffering.

By now, I'd been through 12 different surgeries. For years, my body had been through hell. I'd lost the opportunity for more children, after being prescribed medication that would stop the production of estrogen to battle my cancer. I'd lost my breast, and with that my sense of my own womanhood. I had been beaten, infected, scarred, maimed, wounded. I felt half dead, unable to fight any more battles.

Seven years after my breast cancer, I agreed to a minor surgery to remove scar tissue which was causing discomfort. I could feel my shoulders tense up, at the very mention of this procedure. Soon after the surgery, I found myself right back to taking care of my family, working out and pushing myself, overdoing everything when I should have been resting and taking care of myself.

What I needed wasn't rest; what I needed was an escape button.

We were planning a family trip to Marco Island in Florida. A magical trip, we promised ourselves, a healing trip.

The morning after our arrival, I noticed myself feeling *different*. *I'm just exhausted,* I told myself; I always experienced exhaustion after pushing myself at everything. Nothing was ever half done; I always exceeded anyone's expectations. But today, I was *off;* today was a different kind of exhaustion.

Instead of my normal five-mile run, I found myself lying on a beach chair in my sneakers and shorts. *Just five more minutes,* I told myself, *five minutes and I'll get up.* Yet I wound up falling asleep—unusual behavior for the type-A personality I'd always been. Awakening, I felt shaky, nauseous, dizzy. I left my husband at the pool and headed back to the hotel room, where I became very ill.

In denial I thought, *this can't be happening to me. It must be a virus.* I called my surgeon; he was on vacation, so I spoke with another doctor on-call. He was dismissive, annoyed and ready for our conversation to be over as soon as it started. "There is no way your recent surgery has anything to do with having a virus," he scolded me. Yet my intuition, my inner guidance told me differently, and I immediately called my husband Scott back to the room.

A doctor friend happened to be staying at our hotel. Phoning him, the doctor asked Scott to feel my breast. "See if it's red and hot," he instructed. When Scott examined my reconstructed breast—the one I had finally welcomed as my own—to his horror he saw it was *on fire*.

The next few hours are a fog. I recall being taken to an urgent care facility, then to a hospital. I woke, hearing someone say, "She is very sick, she needs emergency surgery, she will lose her breast again."

The room seemed to freeze, as I heard the next words. I'd been diagnosed with sepsis.

An infection had set in after my minor surgery, and spread to my bloodstream. How was it possible, that I'd gone from a beach chair to death's door in just a few hours?

The story of my life. Nothing could be easy. Everything was hard and complicated and impossible to survive. I knew this time: *I don't have the strength to live.*

I don't remember waking up in the hospital after surgery. Instantly I felt weak; I was having a hard time breathing, I recall telling the nurses and doctors when they arrived. They told me this was normal post-surgery. But this wasn't normal; this was different. I'd had many surgeries before, and this was very different.

After seven days, I still felt like death. "Take me home," I begged Scott; there was nothing the hospital was doing that I could not do for myself. Against doctors' orders, I checked out. Still unable to take a full breath of air in my lungs, I said nothing as my husband wheeled me down the corridor and out the door. I insisted we book the first flight to Philadelphia. It was time to go home.

Returning to our hotel, to await our flight, I realized I probably should never have left the hospital. I felt incredibly woozy. My eyes fluttered and my head began to nod, as if I was falling backward. I told Scott, "I think

I'm dying." He lay me down on the bed, and raced off to find my sister, who was also on vacation with us.

Minutes passed. I lay quietly, my head in my hands, trying to stem the tide of panic. As I lay there, alone, tears streaming, a wave of intense light suddenly enveloped me. The intense warmth I felt was indescribable. I remember floating above my body and seeing myself, weak and terri-fied, lying on the bed. The light brought fleeting memories of the car acci-dent, my first near-death, infusing my soul with the Light. My soul knew the Light. My soul longed for the Light. With all of me, I intended to be back in the Light. I saw myself down below in bed, struggling to breathe, desperately pleading over and over again, *Mother Mary, fill me with your light. Mary, fill me with your light. Mary, fill me with your light.*

As I repeated this, my heart soaking up the Light, I experienced my second near-death.

In the quiet, I followed the beckoning Light. I don't know if it was minutes or hours later, but I found it, I felt it, I was enveloped in it. I moved slowly in what felt like peace and love. The Light was hugging me, comforting me, and holding me as I drifted with it, higher and higher. I saw angels—angels everywhere. It felt like I knew them all, as if I had been to this place before. It felt like home.

I floated in the love and comfort and arms of the Light. As it was with my first near-death experience, I now saw the tunnel. The tunnel yawned wide. The tunnel yawned black. I saw a standing figure in the Light, shaped like a normal human being. And then there he was—Mary's son, Jesus, just as I had always known Him. There was no fear; there was no judgment; there was only pure love. Jesus knew me; I knew Him. His Light was greater than the Light surrounding me.

Light rays shone all around me; I felt protected, safe and loved. I remember looking into the Light and crying, and the Light telling me I must go back, it wasn't time for me to be here, that I still had work to do. I understood: I didn't have to die to be in the Light.

In a state of half-dreaming the Light faded. Everything darkened to a complete absence of the Light.

The trip back through the tunnel back was slow. It was as if I was saying goodbye. The Light had filled me whole, and then sent me back, empowered with the gifts of Spirit. In the Light, in the love, I knew there was more for me to do. I hadn't begun my work; I hadn't yet found what was intended for me.

The Light carried me like a child back to my hotel room. Waking, the room was alive with an invisible essence, an unseen presence, whispering. What I knew now was that I didn't need to die, to be in the Light. I didn't need to die, to connect with healing. I could meditate, and pray, and I could live a life worthy of the connection, worthy of the struggle, to all the Light had called me to live.

To all that is.

Arriving back home in Philadelphia, I was weak and intensely sick. My doctors arranged to meet me at the hospital, where I was placed under immediate medical care. For the next several days I was given IV antibiotics by an infectious diseases team, until I was well enough to go home.

My brain was still in the process of adjusting to life after my second NDE. My confusion deepened, when I found myself crying one day.

I didn't stop crying for three months.

I'll never know what prompted these uninvited tears. I wasn't in pain that first day, or feeling worthless; after my NDE, I'd challenged myself to wake from my lulled state of disconnection, and committed to removing my old foundation of fear and negativity. Finally I sensed I was on the right path with my life—yet one day, the tears just started raining down.

And I couldn't stop them.

Why me? Why does this keep happening to me? Confused, baffled, disturbed, each day I'd wake to a steady stream of tears. Every time someone would ask me, "What's the problem? What's wrong?" I'd cry even harder, because I had no answer.

What was my problem?

The tears were real, filled with sorrow, fear and uncertainty. I remember looking at my husband and whispering, in a desperate voice, "Am I going crazy?"

I could feel myself panic, breathing deeply in and out, waiting for his answer. Even prayer didn't help; alone in my bedroom praying, I found myself sobbing. I would cry in my car, in parking lots, in malls, at dinner, at bedtime. I would cry until I had no more tears left. *I'm losing my mind!* I told myself. *What am I so sad about? Is it because of my NDE—because I've been returned from the Light?*

The possibility hit me that I might never stop crying. I'd lost what little ground I'd made in life. I'd lost Tom, my closest friends, my fragile connections, perhaps my sanity—and realizing that, another flood of tears burst out. Family members whispered their concern to each other. "She's having a nervous breakdown."

Their whispers haunted me. Suddenly I had no safe place. The world around me seemed to crumble. Historically I'd been the strong one, the person others came to when they needed something. I was the savior, the hero to help in any way. Yet their powerhouse was no more. I knew it, they knew it, and so I cried even harder.

What I wanted was for someone to tell me, "It's okay to cry." What I wanted was for someone to hug me and tell me, "This will pass, you'll be okay." I wanted someone to do for me, as I had done for others. Offer no judgement, only comfort. But they couldn't. The Cathy they knew was no longer there. She was a shell of the person they once knew.

I was officially broken. Unable to process my old emotions, my lifetime of suffering and sadness had now become rage. Silent, stewing anger brewed deep within my body. My soul screamed, but could never be heard. There was a voice, but it echoed way down inside. It was a voice that bellowed. A voice that had never spoken up for itself. A voice that shrieked out two words no one could hear.

Help me.

I never had a plan to commit suicide. Yet I began to think that everyone would be better off without me.

I'd spent my entire life trying to make people proud: my parents, Tom's mother, my husband, my children. If I did the right things, if I acted a certain way, if I sacrificed, if I were perfect, if I followed *all the rules,* then surely good things would happen to me.

I had created a life of constant, ceaseless giving, without a moment to receive. Emotionally, spiritually and physically, I was drained.

My life force was fading. I knew I was broken; urging myself to believe otherwise was impossible. *I'll never piece myself back together,* I thought. *I've been losing this battle for years. How could I have missed seeing that my life will never be good?* I wished for death, to be back in the tunnel, being drawn toward the embrace of the Light.

In my heart, I knew these negative thoughts were killing me. I needed to get mentally and emotionally well, or I would die. Yet I had no concept of how to feel better.

By now I was lost in a fog of prescription meds, popping powerful anti-anxiety pills. I told myself, *In six months, I will be better.* I wanted so desperately to get off the medication, to stop smoking, to no longer rely on drinking wine to get me through days and nights, to quell the dark feelings.

But my spirit was weak. The pills were my reminder that I was supposed to suffer. I used the pills as escape—to soothe me, comfort me, save me.

Now I was standing at a crossroads, staring down two narrowing paths, where everything was in shadows. Imagining what lay down each road, I would always see a haze, a fog, not an open road, a bright dawn, a clear picture. There had to be a way out.

My mind made a hard turn, and I made a firm decision. *I will get better. I will be healthy and happy, and live a purposeful life. I will continue being the happy wife and mother—but I want to find more. Do more. Be more.*

I didn't know how I'd do it, but I would live a life without anxiety, tears or fear. I could no longer live that way. I'd find a way to be well, to be happy, without anxiety, and I would be a success, living my best life.

There became no other option.

The decision to heal appeared out of that fog. Facing the fork in the road, I could have gone either way; I could have chosen the easier route, the path downward.

I didn't. I wanted something better for myself. But what?

I want out, my desperate mind blurted. *Out of this old life. I can't do this anymore. I've been waiting so long for somebody to heal me. I want to heal others, help others, serve others. It's time to break this cycle.*

Suddenly the utter ridiculousness of the questions I'd never asked myself came rushing in. *Who am I? What do I want?*

Without hesitation I answered. *I want to become a protector. I want to become a healer.*

As those words formed in my mind, I held my breath. My heart thumped. I teared up, biting my lip, until I could hold my feelings back no longer.

I am not here to suffer, I realized. *I am not here to be a victim.*

I am not here to watch my dreams wither, my body wilt under cancer, to wallow forever in hopelessness and despair.

I am here to rise up and become the person the Light created me to be.

I am here to overcome the shame, the self-blame.

I am here to love on and encourage others, to be a guide, a mentor, a light, a flame of burning hope.

And I am here because there is too much that remains undone in my life.

With sudden clarity, the fog on the path suddenly vanished. Instead of feeling victimized by cancer or my near-death experiences, I felt chosen to turn my eyes to the Light, and follow the Light's plan. Instead of being drawn down a black tunnel, I stood before a road that was wide open, able to see the miles ahead for my life.

At last, it was time.

I'd faced so much adversity already. I'd faced death with Tom. I'd faced breast cancer, and death from sepsis. I'd faced depression and hopelessness. Now my life, and all I'd known—all the sadness, the confusion, the anxiety, the grief—shifted. No longer did I shed old tears; those tears were gone. No longer did I put myself last; instead, I considered myself part of the Light's ongoing message, its universal energy. I yearned to understand the Light, why I had been shown death, and a way back.

Why? I asked the Light. *Why did you save me? What great deeds remain to be done in my life?*

In the silence, the Light answered; and hearing the answer, I experienced my first breath of freedom. True freedom.

The weight of the past slid off me in that moment. My life as a free woman began. I turned myself over in complete surrender to wholeheartedly pursuing a relationship with the Light, to change, to push through no matter how the world beat against me, to endure whatever pain was necessary for my complete transformation, and to claim my freedom.

My work had begun.

I had awakened, and won the battle.

I had shifted the story of my life, from pain to purpose.
I had overcome death, to come to life.

PART TWO

OUT OF THE DARK

6

Breaking Free

THIS WAS MY AWAKENING, MY JOURNEY TO FREEDOM.
Surviving my second NDE pried open my fearful mind and transformed
my broken and bruised heart, in the only way possible: From the inside out.

I'd been a captive to fear, a prisoner to my toxic mind and body—but
my NDE threw the door open on my toxic past and set me free. It was time
to come out of the shadows. After my second NDE, I discovered life. No
more seclusion. No more slavery to emotional drama. No more destructive
clinging to the past, or hiding in the darkness—quivering, weak-kneed,
retreating from life, always afraid of being transported down the long
tunnel toward the threshold of death. I had been at the crossroads, seen
an open road leading in all directions, considered my options, and now
I'd chosen my next path.

I had broken through.

I wasn't just alive; I had risen tall on my own two feet. Taking a deep breath, I listened to the pounding of my heart, beating out a new rhythm.

I. Am. Free.

But am I? I still found myself wondering. I could feel the sickness in my mind refusing to fade, rolling through me in great waves. Knowing it would be fatal to give in to it now, I pulled myself together, my heart skipping a beat as the answer I'd sought forever burst out.

I am free!

I am, I am, I am!

An intense rush of emotion surged through me. For a moment, I felt as if my body had been transported somewhere else—as if I'd been awakened from a death-like sleep. Breaking through the debilitating lies in my head that had held me back, I'd escaped the recurring nightmare of Tom's accident. Now it was time to begin the long, grueling process of breaking away from the darkness, the shadows, the wreckage that still lay scattered in the ditch of my past. It was time to embrace the freeing affirmation of Spirit. It was time to pursue my only purpose in life, and to wear that truth on my heart forever.

It was time to choose the Light.

We all have a story. I shake my head in wonder now, looking back at mine. Only true brokenness could have unshackled me from the past and allowed me to overcome a horrific car accident, breast cancer when I was a young mother with babies, then advanced sepsis—to be wounded physically, emotionally, mentally and spiritually, and yet to survive. Only by facing these major obstacles was I able to find freedom.

Freedom can only take root and grow in the unfailing love of the Light.

But what is the Light?

My words can't come close to describing it. In the past, when challenging events occurred in my life, when I was filled with darkness, it was like a bomb imploded, and my sense of self was shattered into pieces. I lost my Light—my self-worth, my self-love, and my voice. Over the course of years, I grew darker, I retreated in defeat, and the negative emotions of shame and guilt took over.

It was after my second NDE that I experienced the profound incident with the Light—the Light we are transported into and become when we cross-over. A gentle wave of pure love flowed through me, flooding my every cell, and I became the Light itself. The Light felt forgiving; the Light was comfort; the Light was peace. It was a feeling I'd longed for my entire life, without even knowing. In the Light during my NDE, the feeling was an intense oneness, as if everyone I met was made of the same Light.

After my NDE, I ached for that Light to return. I longed for its unconditional love; within the Light, as I slipped further and further from consciousness, further away from my day-to-day suffering, my darkness was released, a feeling of bliss came flooding through me, and my mind radiated clarity.

But back to my question: *What is the Light?*

The Light is you. The Light is me. The Light is love. The Light is the Divine. The Light calls us to a place of breaking free. Opening our hearts to it—filling our minds with its peace, and feeling the Light growing more powerful within—we can become the Light.

When I was sick with PTSD and anxiety, and taking heavy doses of prescription medications—Concerta for ADHD, Zoloft for depression, Ativan for anxiety—my family would whisper to each other behind my back, thinking I was out of earshot. "She is taking too many meds…and it's making her crazy!"

They were right. My mind was cracking. I was having a nervous breakdown. Circumstances overwhelmed me. Family members could see it, and it made them uncomfortable and frightened. Their worry and concern drove me even deeper into isolation and filled me with shame.

Tormented by shame, my body shivered and shook, trying to release the guilt that had ravaged me with illness and disease. *This is guilt I'll carry for the rest of my life,* I realized in horror—yet I couldn't help but feel beset with ugly shame for the part I'd played in embarrassing my family.

One day, in utter desperation, I stumbled to my computer, trembling hands Googling the words *How to heal.* Clicking on the first link, I was taken to a site for the author and energy healer Deborah King. Reading her story—how her life was radically changed with a cancer diagnosis; how she conquered drug and alcohol addictions; and how she healed herself, her addictions, her cancer, and her life wounds—I was amazed and inspired. *If she can do it, I can do it, too!*

I signed up for every course the Deborah King site offered—Chakra Wisdom, Learning to Meditate, and LifeForce Energy Healing® among them. The life-healing she offered required my willingness to stop suppressing my pain and old trauma—to see, to feel, to release my pain and to let it go. It took time—months of work on myself—but armed with Deborah's teaching I released my old self-limiting beliefs and allowed the energy of the Light to take over.

And I slowly healed.

It was during this period of intense study that I began spending more and more time alone again—in silence, in healing, in nature. As a child, I'd always had a fond place in my heart for the natural world—for clouds and sky, roaring rivers and streams, trees, plants, birds, insects, animals. Once again, I felt drawn to connect with this world.

Each day, I would take silent walks into nature, intending to connect with whatever wildlife or flora came my way. One day, I spied a tiny red clover, sprouting up through the cracks in the street. The beauty of this tenacious little flower rising through the concrete stopped me in my tracks—bending over, I acknowledged the dogged resolve and fearlessness of that tiny clover. In my head, I was startled to suddenly hear this flower's reply. *You too, can get through,* it said. *You too, can make it.* In surprise, I laughed out loud to myself—I felt vaguely ridiculous for actually having a conversation with this clover, and for realizing how absolutely crazy I'd appear to my family and friends!

These walks became my greatest healing time. Each day, the trees and animals I encountered would send me a message—sometimes in the way a leaf fell, other times in the whisper of a warm summer breeze. Everything spoke to me—telling me I could grow my own way, just like the tree that curved to the side, bending its trunk around a telephone pole, yet continuing to grow tall. Like the tree, I could move past every obstacle in my way. Like the tree, my imperfections would become my perfections.

But it was one particular tree—a humble, old Ash tree—that gave me the greatest message of all.

Since high school, I'd been a runner. Not because I ran on the school track team—I just enjoyed the exercise, the freedom, the effortless sensation of my body in action. I liked the feeling of accomplishment running gave me—but I also coveted the solitude, the serenity, the quiet. While running, my sneakered feet slapping the pavement, I was able to check out, to be alone with my thoughts, my head free of fear, my mind at peace. I liked that.

I became a workout fanatic. Wanting to finish my workouts fast, I knew if I walked for miles it would take me an hour, but if I ran it would take me much less. I ran half marathons, always hoping to complete a full one. But life and the surgeries got in the way, and I stopped running, putting it aside for six years.

It was after my initial healing work that I returned to running. Running now became a form of moving meditation. I'd run every day—4 miles most days, 3 miles others. As I ran, my energy field expanded with each cleansing breath, and I became lost in the flowing air, the silence, the path ahead and the sky above. I became part of Mother Nature's scenery, like the chattering squirrels and baby robins my gliding body swooped by, like the trees that whispered and gently spoke to me.

I never noticed her, the Queen of the Ash trees, until the day she spoke to me.

I was exhausted that day, feeling weak and run-down. The healing process is hard; there are good days and bad days, and this day I was feeling lost, disconnected. So disconnected, in fact, that I was contemplating going back to healing the old way, with some Ativan. *Going back to the old ways would be easier,* my tired mind pleaded, *than the hard work of actually feeling, and healing. Why don't you try it?*

As I ran that day, wondering if I had tucked away a bottle of Ativan somewhere, I came upon a towering old tree completely covered in twisting green vines. I'm certain I'd passed this tree before on my runs—it was in a protected wildlife area near a small creek that ran sweetly over rocks— yet on this day something about it caught my eye. Its trunk was majestic, wizened with age, yet towering high overhead and nearly eclipsing the sun. And though its limbs were nearly choked under strangling vines—vines as thick as my arm—her limbs reached outward in a gesture of welcoming acceptance toward the sky.

How strangely beautiful, I thought, stopping on the trailside to get a better glimpse. In my mind I found myself asking the tree how it took care of all those vines. "How do you do it?" I said aloud, as if speaking to someone in the flesh. As I continued running, a voice came from the tree, echoing far above my head.

I have enough, the voice answered. *I have enough of the sun. I have enough of the healing moon. I take the nutrients from the ground, and I soak up the water from the dewy leaves. At times during the day,* the tree went on, *I still the branches and quiet the leaves. And sometimes, I tell a vine to find another tree to cling to, and it always does.*

I have enough, said the tree.

I blinked, in shock, nearly jumping out of my skin. The tree *knew* me. The tree knew I hadn't enough. She knew I was weak, I was tired, I was overwhelmed. I was taking on too much, over-doing and under-achieving, living without joy, without boundaries. The tree knew I lacked nutrients—the water, the quiet, the sun, the moon. I needed to take care of me, and not become strangled by the weight of my own vines.

The tree knew.

I stared upward, my mind racing, my shoulders heaving up and down as I tried to slow my breath. Our meeting had been timed perfectly. As I continued my run, my thoughts blurring, I kept thinking back to that old tree. I felt her energy and her love, her branches reaching out and embracing me tight. That day, she became a part of me—my guide, my caretaker, a mother, in a way.

Years later, I was grieving the loss of my 15-year-old dog Dolly. Through all my ups and down in life, through all my surgeries and recoveries, Dolly had laid by my side—my best friend, my protector. Now she was gone, and I longed for her physical presence, her love. I wanted the warmth of Dolly's fur under my hand. I craved our silent conversations, our secret knowledge, the adventures we'd shared.

Distraught, I decided to run from my grief. In terrible pain I bolted from the house, and I ran. Deeper and deeper into the forest I ran, feeling the tunnel of darkness at my heels, waiting to open up and shut me in again. *Keep it together, just keep it together,* I pleaded with myself, tears stinging my eyelids. As I plunged into a clearing, and saw my mother Ash tree farther up the trail, I began to openly cry. Just as a child would cry for their mother, I wept—sobbing, wailing, wishing I could be cradled in her branches.

"Please," I begged her, running into her open arms, "please, take this grief from me! Take my sorrow!"

As I spoke those words to her, a choir of voices came from the forest all around me.

We are, I heard them all say. *We are taking it,* the trees whispered. *All of it.*

And they did. They took the pain, the sadness, the sorrow. They took the weight of the grief, the sorrow I could not let go of. For perhaps the first time since my NDE, I didn't feel alone. I sensed the Light's presence in these trees. I knew the Light was here, watching over me, with me.

I knew the Light would heal me. Even if I didn't know *why.*

It was in meditation that I eventually found the Light again—the same Light I had found in Tom's car after the accident. In meditation, I found the same Light that blinded me with love, when I experienced sepsis. In meditation, I realized that the peace, the unconditional love I found in both of my NDEs was available to me, here on earth. I did not have to die again, to live. I did not have to die again, to be bathed in the love and the Light.

Learning to meditate was a process. When I first began meditating, my entire body would be physically affected, as if I were being rocked by a slow-moving spasm. I experienced the grief, the pain, the negative emotions leaving my body. Each time, I sensed the dark emotions being released from my sick mind, while joy and liberation poured through me. It felt like I was climbing the staircase to Divine Light. The more I healed, the higher I rose on the staircase; the higher I climbed, the more I heard, saw and understood my purpose.

Over time, my meditation changed. I began seeing a bright Light in meditation, which seemed to draw closer to me the more I meditated. It was like living a near-death experience every day—the same bright Light, the same angelic music. Once again, I felt myself drawn away from the earthly realm, guided by this presence with a sense of urgency to reach me. I felt at home. In the silence of meditation, time stopped. I ceased worrying, agonizing, panicking—there were no expectations, no drama, no conflicts, only surprise, love, joy.

In meditation, everything was perfect. In meditation, I was running into the arms my mother tree, running into the arms of the Light. My struggles were still out there, waiting for my return. But with meditation, it was possible to know peace and pain at the same time. Though I still hated pain and suffering, I thanked the Light for a way to bypass it, for the gift preparing me for the *next* world, while making my priority *this* world, this life.

But the greatest gift the Light granted was the opportunity to be me. And to allow me, Cathy, the choice to come back to this life, and heal.

At first, I began to study energy healing to heal myself.

It began with the discovery of a mass in my groin area. Consulting with two specialists, I was advised to have the mass biopsied. I freaked out. *No way am I having another surgery!* my desperate mind protested.

Searching for alternatives to traditional medicine, I discovered two unconventional allies: an alternative doctor who'd studied food intolerances, and an acupuncturist. Placing my fate in their hands, over the next few months I was shocked to watch as the mass slowly shrunk, then faded, then disappeared. I was healed—no surgery, no drugs, no cutting of tissue!

I was shocked. How to explain this miracle? Beyond understanding, I spent the next months studying to heal myself. Slowly I stopped taking my anxiety medication, replacing it with meditation and time spent in nature. I also learned to clear my chakras every day. I journaled, taking the time to get to know myself better, without judgment or shame, discovering my deepest truths and honoring my core beliefs.

Suddenly I had an awareness about myself I'd never experienced. As I continued to grow and change and heal spiritually, emotionally and physically, I began to sense my true power and my purpose. Miraculously, the black cloud of toxic smoke that seemed to block my view of life had finally disappeared. The sun dawned differently; the moon waxed in new, unfamiliar ways. Birds sang and spoke in voices I'd never encountered. In the pale light of morning, I could raise my eyes to a tree and bend my ear to a flower, and know their presence was divine and inspiring.

For months on end, this new vision of life both amazed me, and drove me to tears. As I healed, I went back to the hard times in my life—not to relive them, but to retrieve *me*. I reclaimed parts of myself I'd abandoned along the road leading up to Tom's accident. I let go of the guilt of surviving, the shame of moving on. I forgave myself for bringing breast cancer into my home. Returning to the moment I experienced sepsis in the hospital, learning I was going to lose the breast I had just regained, I said goodbye to the breast once and for all, and goodbye to the PTSD that went with it.

Most importantly, I allowed myself to live by the beliefs that aligned with my core, my purpose. *No longer will I be afraid of who I am,* I boldly told myself. *No longer will I be afraid to admit I've had two near-death experiences—because with them, I received the gifts of compassion, of understanding, of teaching and leading. And I won't be afraid to tell people that I work on behalf of Spirit, helping others become their greatest, most divine selves.*

I can say these things, I told myself, *and I can move forward. I can still live.*

I have healed.

Becoming a healer for others was the next step.

I remember the day I opened the door to my energy healing practice. That first day, a client sat next to me on the couch, trying to string together her problem in half-babbled sobs. "I woke up crying," she moaned, "and I haven't stopped crying since!"

In that moment, I knew. I was just where I needed to be.

The clarity that came with my own healing allowed me to see myself in others, and them in me. I would sit with these people, suffering with them, crying with them, holding them, hugging them, waiting for their panic to pass. There would never be an *AHHH-HA* moment for someone in a state of anxiety, depression, or grieving; it just was not possible. It was in the silence, in the calm, that my words could be heard.

So that is where I began. In the silence. For I understood silence. I spoke silence.

In the silence, when the calm came, I explained how I was able to heal my anxiety, depression and PTSD. Healing would not happen overnight, I warned them; it would take time, and an enormous amount of conviction, passion and work. But it would happen, if they committed to it.

"You will fall," I told them, "and you will have to get back up. Then you will fall again, and again, and you will have to get back up. And each time you need to pick yourself up again, it will get easier and easier, until it becomes effortless. "

"One day," I promised, "you will wake up with no more pain. Only peace, and purpose. But only if you do the work."

Still, words are a poor tool. Often these people wanted a quick fix, a cure, a remedy. What was the magic potion?

"It's *you*," I told them. "*You*, the person needing healing. It's up to you to decide—with an unbending intent—that it is time to heal. Every day, you must remember that intent and see the intent and live with the intent to heal. You must see yourself healing, accept the possibility of freedom on the other side—living without the worry, the shame or the guilt of it all.

"One day, things will change," I promised. As their minds processed these words, I'd watch their lips form into a slight but unmistakable smile. Smiling back, as if to confirm we hadn't imagined it, I watched as tears of joy began to flow. Then I'd walk them to the door, at perhaps the longest day of their lives, knowing that for right now, for today, that was enough.

Clarity and peace had finally found me, filled me, healed me. I was no longer trapped in my own cage of near-death—I'd finally walked through the gate. Finding the Light allowed me to put pieces of myself together in a way that would challenge me, test me, and guide me, for the rest of my life.

Healing others would be my cloth. To practice and write and teach on energy healing and the power of the Light would be my calling. The distressed, the disturbed, the lost, the traumatized—these would be my brothers and sisters.

I would live each day, renewed, restored, free of anxiety, depression and PTSD.

I would live each day, a healer.

In the end, I became passionate about life because of death—my near-death, my NDEs. My NDEs changed me. My NDEs transformed me, helping me to grow and develop. Acknowledging my NDEs saved me, propelled me, cleansed me. Speaking openly about my near-death experiences broke free the chains of my stigma—suddenly everything that had happened to me on that dark highway in 1988 made sense. My future no longer seemed as uncertain as that pitch-black road that once lay ahead of me.

Patiently, lovingly my NDEs had led me to this point in my journey, to this moment. To the place I now called home.

But what *is* an NDE? Why do some of us experience negative near-death episodes, and others the bliss of heavenly release? And if there is life after an NDE, why do we try to hide our experiences with near-death, the revelation of a next world, like a guilty secret?

7

What is an NDE?

WHAT IS IT LIKE TO DIE? TO EXPERIENCE DEATH? HAVE SURVI-
vors of an NDE truly experienced death? Does an NDE provide a window
into death, into the next world, into the after-life—or is it only an altered
reality, a transcendent state of the imagination?

What exactly *is* an NDE?

The phrase "near-death experience" (or NDE) first came into popu-
lar use in psychologist Raymond Moody's 1976 book, *Life After Life*.
Moody proposed that those experiencers coming close to death undergo
a profound, consciousness-altering episode, in which they seem to leave
their bodies and enter another realm. Returning from this dimension
often led NDErs to make transformative changes in their personal beliefs,
their outlook on life, and their core values—but also left many disturbed,
disoriented, tormented by too many unexplained questions. Telling others
about their experience often led survivors to be stigmatized, discredited,

plagued with relationship problems, to turn to addiction and isolation, to become humiliated and pathologically depressed.

When I found the courage to tell people about my own near-death experiences, I was shocked by their disinterest and apathy. In most cases, I never ventured deep enough into the conversation to explain in detail what had occurred. Over time I realized it was best for me to keep the most unbelievable details to myself.

In the past, like so many others who'd experienced a brush with death and an invitation to the Light, I kept my experience secret, fearing listeners would think me out of my mind or telling a story that is too incredible.

This is the unfortunate reality of surviving an NDE. The experience itself can be traumatic, or it can be blissful—liberating the NDEr from their normal perception or life or imprisoning them in an otherworldly phenomenon they can never understand.

Generally speaking, there are 15 common characteristics of an NDE. They include feelings of peace; being transported down a long dark tunnel; facing a border or a point of no return; a sensation of floating, of being outside of their own body; meeting with celestial or malevolent beings; the acquiring of knowledge the experiencer wouldn't acquire through normal perception; and being returned to life.

These features have defined the near-death experience for decades—some would claim for centuries. If so, how has it escaped logical explanation, or a simple interpretation? How many people have experienced an NDE?

Recent studies claim that approximately 1 in 10 of us have undergone a near-death experience. I tend to believe the number might be higher—I myself didn't realize the incidents in Tom's car accident and in my near-death from sepsis were in fact NDEs. Only years later did I understand and accept the undeniable truth.

How does an NDE happen? What triggers an NDE?

Circumstances differ. Cardiac arrest, rapid loss of blood, electrocution, near drownings, auto accidents, traumatic injuries to the brain and suicide attempts are situations that often trigger an NDE. On the verge of death, loss of consciousness or subjected to a traumatic or unpleasant life event, one may experience the presence of a bright light, the sensation of being transported down a tunnel, toward a destination unknown.

Regardless of the circumstances, every experiencer speaks of a similar occurrence.

The list is expansive, but the similarities are striking, and the thread of each NDEr's experience nearly universal—always there is the sudden transport down a tunnel, and the meeting with the Light, being enveloped by unbelievable warmth and love; for others, the experience in the Light seems to indicate a frightening dead-end, a spinning vortex into doom or the abyss, or a point of no return.

Artistic depictions of near-death run the gamut also, and can be traced back centuries. Heironymus Bosch's painting *Ascent of the Blessed* portrays benevolent winged beings, heavenly clouds, and an intensely-bright light at the end of a long tunnel. More recently, in the film *Heaven Is For Real* (based upon a true story), a young boy returns from his NDE and identifies the face of Jesus—painted by a 4-year-old Lithuanian girl—as the vision he saw while transported to Heaven.

Comparing NDE reports from other countries and cultures suggests that cultural beliefs may have a profound influence on a person's account following a close brush with near-death. Cross-cultural differences and religious beliefs may affect a survivor's account or retelling of their NDE— this suggests that though the experience itself may be similar or universal, the way NDErs interpret their near-death and return to life can be singular and unique to each individual.

Some researchers believe that NDEs are by-products of our imagination, our dreams and nightmares, our brain protecting itself from having to face the fear and threat of imminent or imagined death.

Through more than 40 years of NDE research, through thousands upon thousands of interviews with NDErs, a limited number of personal traits or variables have been shown to predict who will have an NDE, or what kind of experience one may have. Recent studies suggest that experiencers may be more prone to hypnotic states or transcendent states of reality than others; they may recall childhood trauma more easily, may recollect and recount their dreams more vividly. Whether these traits are alike because of the subjects experiencing an NDE, or whether those subjects already displaying these characteristics are more likely to experience NDEs, is so far a mystery.

The science of NDEs is even trickier. What causes an NDE? What triggers the body and mind to transcend the boundaries of our understanding, and come close to death?

Medical researchers assert it is all a matter of chemistry, of bad biology: a shortage of oxygen to the brain, or altered blood gases, toxic or metabolic hallucinations or the body's neurochemical response to severe impairment, to intense fear and trauma. Those who have experienced an NDE dismiss these claims by the medical community. Inadequate, untrue, too easy, they say. The experience itself is too mystical, the journey to death's door too supernatural, the number of NDE cases too diverse and wide-ranging to consistently explain the phenomenon.

Ever since Raymond Moody's seminal book was published and reached worldwide acclaim in the 1970s, the study and investigation into death and NDEs has multiplied immensely, and become a branch of science all its own.

In an inquiry titled *Near-Death Experiences: The Basics* by Nancy Evans Bush, President of the International Association for Near-Death Studies, and Bruce Greyson, Professor of Psychiatry & Neurobehavioral Sciences at the University of Virginia, the incidence of negative NDEs was analyzed. Three kinds of responses to a distressing or disturbing NDE were documented: *the inverse, the void,* and *the hellish.*

The Inverse NDE found subjects reporting the opposite of most experiencers—what the majority of NDErs described as blissful or pleasurable, those suffering an Inverse NDE recounted as nightmarish, hostile, threatening. Instead of being benignly transported into warm and loving white light, these NDErs felt themselves shooting at incredible speed past shadowy beings, or deceased family members. The bizarre and unsettling experience left them panic-stricken, overcome with sadness and often afflicted with bouts of severe depression.

The Void NDE subjects described being transported from their bodies to a vast and forbidding blackness, an emptiness. There, they experienced a devastating feeling of loneliness, fearful isolation, and often personal annihilation. Subjects reported being told by unseen entities that their life on Earth never was, that they had never been born, never existed. Left alone in the emptiness of black space, they continued plunging into a dark abyss, their silent screams sucked into this cosmic nothingness.

The Hellish NDE experiencer appears to be the least common. They recount falling endlessly into the depths of the Earth, where they are bombarded by visions of malevolent presences—"horrific beings with gray gelatinous appendages grasping and clawing at me," reports one interviewed subject. Others perceive wandering souls and wailing spirits, who appear lost and groaning in agonizing pain, and a faceless guide welcoming them to the gates of Hell. In the Hellish NDE, there is no means of escape, no embrace by the Light, nothing beautiful or pleasant—only the grotesque, the ugly, and agony.

The authors also document three common varieties of NDE responses described by subjects, calling these responses *the turnaround, reductionism*, and *the long haul.*

The turnaround is described as "the classic response to a profound spiritual experience—a conversion, the changing of one's spiritual bent or religion." This frightening response to an NDE is interpreted by subjects as a threat, a warning, a premonition that they must "turn their life around." Responses to this warning are radical. Atheists thrust into a negative NDE frequently become devout Christians, or attend seminary school; drug-abusers stop using drugs, and enter a Bible college; hard-core criminals opt for a life of helping others, embracing the existence of a deity. All sense they have been returned from a terrifying situation and been given a second chance, vowing now to dedicate their lives to a Higher Power.

Reductionism subjects, unable to fit their experience into any category, treat their NDE as if it never happened, as if the incident doesn't matter. They rationalize and dismiss the NDE into simpler elements: their brain was under too much stress; lack of oxygen interrupted the normal function of their visual cortex; their mind was "tricked" into misinterpreting some optical illusion as a tunnel and blinding white lights. Any unanswered questions remain unanswered, or go unaddressed. They conclude it was all a hallucination, not a normal reaction to trauma, not a perceived reality—and certainly not an NDE. Masking their unanswered questions with science, they do nothing to resolve them.

The long haul subjects all exhibit immense difficulty comprehending their NDE, struggling in its aftermath. Baffled, they pepper themselves with questions: "What did I do to deserve this? Why *me?*" Unable to integrate their NDE into anything logical, they are filled with absolute terror. Repressing the memory isn't possible; it feels too real, too vivid to forget. The incident is too disturbing and potentially humiliating to even discuss with their loved ones. Decades later, unable to get it out of their heads, they will continue to struggle with their experience, with its implications, and will search until their deathbeds for a reasonable explanation.

Decades after Moody's book struck an emotional chord and kick-started an entire new branch of scientific and theological study, the scientific community continues trying to understand NDEs, to interpret their meaning and purpose. Is it elevated spirituality? A vision of Heaven? An altered reality?

Those of us who have experienced an NDE know the reality, the benefits and the burdens, all too well.

Many NDErs find a heightened sense of purpose, a greater compassion for others, a rebirth of their self-awareness. They find their experience similar to the "Supreme Union" described in the *Tibetan Book of the Dead*, where the experiencer becomes dissolved into his or her true nature, purified and merged into the "Clear Light" of an infinite being.

Many NDErs report this perception of being merged with the Light. In the *Tibetan Book of the Dead*, the Clear Light makes its appearance after death, merging with the experiencer into transcendent oneness. This oneness with the Clear Light is seen as the basis of enlightenment, the awakening of the true nature of the experiencer's mind. The experiencer no longer has any sense of a separate identity; they are the Light, one with the Light.

I was one with the Light. In my NDE, the Light and I were in union. The Light was transcendent love, a liberation from fear. The Light was home.

In the *Tibetan Book of the Dead*, the experience of dying awakens the experiencer to a homecoming, a new reality of love, peace, awareness, compassion. The secret message of the universe is revealed to be love, the most essential quality in life. In this aspect, the *Tibetan Book of the Dead* and the experience of near-death are united, illuminating their message not on death or dying, not on fear of the next life or the next world, but on the renewal and resurrection of *this* life, on the reality of how we human beings should live our lives.

But what message *is* an NDE trying to send us? Near-death incidents recounted by famed novelist Ernest Hemingway are one example of the possible central message of an NDE.

In 1918, during the first World War, Hemingway was wounded by exploding shrapnel. The explosion knocked Hemingway unconscious and buried him in the earth of his Army dugout. Two soldiers standing between Hemingway and the shell's impact were not so fortunate; one died instantly, and the other had both of his legs severed and died days later.

Hospitalized in Milan, Italy, Hemingway wrote home to his family: "Dying is a very simple thing. I've looked at death, and I know."

Decades later, the author explained his cryptic remark to a friend.

"A big Austrian trench mortar bomb, of the type that used to be called ash cans, exploded in the darkness. I died then. I felt my soul or something coming right out of my body, like you'd pull a silk handkerchief out of a pocket by one corner. It flew around and then came back and went in again and I wasn't dead anymore."

Up until his death by suicide in 1961, Hemingway remained deeply impacted by his near-death experience. In his classic war novel *A Farewell To Arms,* the book's hero undergoes the same transformation after encountering death from an exploding bomb: "There was a flash, as when a blast-furnace door is swung open, and a roar that started white and went red and on and on in a rushing wind. I tried to breathe but my breath would not come and I felt myself rush bodily out of myself and out and out and out and all the time bodily in the wind. I went out swiftly, all of myself, and I knew I was dead and that it had all been a mistake to think you just died. Then I floated, and instead of going on I felt myself slide back. I breathed and I was back."

Experiencing premonitions of danger—feeling torn between the two planes of existence—is what I experienced during sepsis. Much like Ernest Hemingway's account, I saw myself floating above my own body, undergoing what is commonly known in the NDE community as an *out-of-body experience* (or OBE).

An out-of-body experience is described as the sensation of floating, or flying, of leaving behind your physical body. The term was first coined in 1943 as an alternative to out-of-consciousness episodes such as astral projection, or "spirit-walking." OBEs are triggered by traumatic brain injuries, psychedelic drugs, dehydration, sleep deprivation, and dreaming, among other causes. It's estimated that 1 in 13 Americans have experienced an OBE—many experiencing episodes several times.

An example is an OBE incident involving Jazmyne Cidavia-DeRepentigny of Hull, Georgia. Her OBE occurred as she lay dying on the operating table during surgery.

"I was floating over my body," DeRepentigny recalled years later. "I could see and hear everything that was being said and done. I knew why I'd died: it was because I couldn't breathe. There was a tube down my throat and the medical staff did not have an oxygen mask on my nose. I had also been given too much anesthetic." In her out-of-body state, DeRepentigny used her mind to make her arm and hand move, trying to pull the tube out of her mouth. Her persistence to make an arm move finally paid off; seeing her movement, the attendants quickly pulled the tube out, an oxygen mask was attached, and her breathing resumed.

Cidavia-DeRepentigny experienced another OBE at age 13, and again years later, after a near-fatal battle with pneumonia. During this episode, she saw herself as a "helpless spirit" residing outside of her body. "I could see my spirit standing before me," she recounts. "My spirit was so beautifully perfect, dressed in a white gown that was loose, free-flowing, and below the knee. From my spirit there emanated a bright, soft-white halo. It was so strange, for I could see my spirit and my spirit could see my pathetic body. My spirit felt warm and so, so celestial. As my spirit slowly moved away, my spirit told my body goodbye, for my spirit saw the light and wanted to go into it. The light was like a circular opening that was warm and bright."

Cidavia-DeRepentigny grieved over the few people she could safely share her OBE episodes with—a typical experience, for many NDErs. For many years, she experienced confusion and disorientation from her OBEs, wishing she could have followed the pull to unite her spirit with the Light.

Another out-of-body theory makes the act of dying or coming face-to-face with death analogous with the experience of birth—replaying the moment when we emerge through the birth canal, into the light of the world. This "birth memory" theory was popularized by the astronomer Carl Sagan, who interpreted near-death experiences as a remembrance of one's day of birth.

Comparing birth to death, the common features are indeed striking. I felt strongly during my NDE that I was being "reborn," as I was guided lovingly back to life. Perhaps the NDE is an incorporation of both experiences—birth and death, the blissful and the frightening.

Hearing the unsettling or sometimes demonic stories about NDEs can be frightening. Unfortunately for those who experience a negative NDE, there can be long-lasting trauma.

Though most NDErs adjust, many struggle to understand their experience. Doubting their sanity, afraid of rejection or severe alienation should they share their story with unbelievers, they struggle with an inability to function in the "real" world, and hesitate to seek help.

Family issues often arise, as the NDEr adopts new values, new interests, new beliefs. Friends avoid or reject the NDEr, seeing his changed behavior as strange, his new perspective on life bizarre or unrealistic.

Emotional issues frequently arise after an NDE. Most often they include anger and frustration at being returned to life against the experiencer's will. Some drop their lifelong traditional religious beliefs, their old life suddenly having no meaning, struggling to redefine what is "normal," coming to define their life by their NDE. Ridiculed by family and friends, they become gloomy and depressed, or alienated, and turn to drugs or alcohol for escape and comfort, no longer able to accept the limitations of friendships, their marriage, or any other relationships.

As their NDE becomes disruptive to the family, it's no surprise that the divorce rate among NDErs is higher than the average population.

Broken relationships, severe alienation, disrupted careers and long-term depression—the difficult adjustments to life after an NDE sometimes lead experiencers to suicidal thoughts, as they "romanticize" death. On the other hand, many NDErs appear to have less death anxiety than non-NDErs, and see death as less threatening after their episode. They feel enhanced by the meaningfulness and joy of living.

Most experiencers report incredibly pleasant happenings in the Light, however. For many like myself, the benefits and blessings outweigh the burden of surviving an NDE.

The most frequently-stated benefit of a positive NDE is the experience of a blissful, profound sensation of peace and love. They feel their fear replaced by security, serenity. NDErs often share positive stories about floating above their body during an NDE, and witnessing their "dying" physical body below. Some recount the experience of meeting angels, and communicating with benevolent beings—often telepathically—while some report having loving conversations with deceased loved ones or ancestors.

And of course, every NDEr remembers the Light—bright, warm and all-encompassing. What the Light teaches is for each NDEr to reflect upon themselves.

Other positive side-effects include a decreased fear of death, an increased spirituality, a deeper appreciation of life and a heightened concern and compassion for others. A lessened desire for material things also comes after an NDE, as the experiencer's values and attitudes have been forever altered.

Earlier we spoke about merging with the Light. Theories about negative NDEs often come down to the concept of surrender—NDErs battling the Light, resisting the Light, refusing to merge or to be drawn in.

The idea of surrender may be a factor. Those who do submit and surrender control to the Light seem to find a more uplifting phenomenon than those refusing to "let go," fighting the experience so fiercely that it becomes a battle for survival, an escape *from* connecting with the Light, rather than a radiant moment of freedom.

Regardless of your experience, life after an NDE can feel isolating, even knowing that many others have experienced a similar event. In interviews, those who've come back from an NDE report they are much happier, more compassionate people, with less fear of death or the unknown. They see the world through a new lens, and are less affected by things that once bothered them. For the most part, people experiencing an NDE come back sensing they have an important purpose in life. Even those who experienced near-death during a suicide attempt often report that they long to live again, realizing the value and importance of life and the fact that they've been given a second chance.

NDEs have provided us with a glimpse of the "other side," of what life is like in the Light: a place filled with unconditional love, compassion and peace. A place filled with all that we would hope life-after-life would be.

In this chapter, we've defined and described the elements of a typical NDE, and interpreted some of its possible meanings. In the next chapters, we'll discuss four of the negative side-effects of an NDE: Anxiety, addiction, post-traumatic stress disorder—

And depression.

8

Depression After an NDE

SUICIDE.

The word kept popping into my head. My scalp tingled and itched, my breathing fast and shallow each time the word came to me.

Suicide.

My head was crawling with the word. The word screamed so loud I couldn't think. I collapsed on the mattress, shivering under the covers, dissolving into tears as the word looped in my brain. *Suicide? That's something sick, desperate people do,* my mind blurted out. I felt my heart quickening, my body fighting off the sweats, my stomach muscles clenching into a tight fist each time the word infiltrated my brain.

Suicide.

Locked inside my bedroom as if it were a cage, I crawled further under the covers, my worn-out mind straining for sanity. Wracked by waves of foreboding thoughts, I tried to pinpoint the moment the thought of suicide had first come to me. *How did I get here?* I wondered. *Where did the idea come from?*

I never thought of *how* I would commit suicide; I never plotted it out. I just remember the word materializing to me one day out of nowhere, speaking softly to me, buzzing gently in my brain. The first time it came, I felt tidal waves of panic swell within me. I wrestled with the word, furious at myself—yet I'd been depressed for so long that every cell in my body was numb. I was coming apart. Considering ending my life just seemed like a natural extension of the nightmare I was living.

The second time it came, I was driving in my car. Even though it was a bright and sunny day, I'd been bombarded all morning by doom-filled thoughts. Maybe it was the church, the shining cross under the bright light of the sun—or maybe just the hopeful message on the church sign outside that changed my mood. Maybe it was neither, just my soul saying, *No. No you won't*—while my dark mind argued, *Yes. Yes.* I knew in those moments that my soul spoke louder than my negative thoughts—I knew that could and would never happen.

I would never think of it again. It was as if the dormant warrior in my soul rose up louder, and my Spirit within me moved and screamed at me to find help, before it was too late.

I still get goosebumps when I think about how close I came to suicide. It came from looking at my life through the lens of depression. Broken pieces. Terrible choices. Ugly future. That was the dominating portrait depression painted of me.

Most people had no idea I was depressed; I hid it well. I would put on my best game face, make myself appear right to the world and everyone around me. Then I would trudge home, sweat pearling on my scalp, lock the bedroom door and sink fast to the floor, after giving the last ounce of energy I had.

Surviving is only the beginning, in life after near-death.

Guilt, shame, nightmares, anxiety, post-traumatic stress, depression, thoughts of suicide…these issues are the reality for many survivors of an NDE.

Depression after an NDE is not unusual. Brought back to life after my NDEs, I begged and pleaded to be returned to the Light. Nothing could lift me out of the depression of being brought back to the world. Each day felt dark, and even my feverish prayers couldn't pierce that darkness. I wanted to stay in the Light, the place of unconditional love and peace. Had I been rejected by the Light? Why wasn't I worthy of it? Had I let my Source down? How had I failed in my life?

These questions haunted me, hounded me, led me to feelings of isolation, loneliness and uncertainty. Once again, I questioned my self-worth. Coming back through that tunnel of light to the world was like moving from a warm, cozy fire to a brutally-cold wintery storm. I should have been thankful to be back; on the one hand, I had survived near-death and I was alive with my family. I should have been grateful—but I couldn't stop thinking about the voice I heard. "My daughter Cathleen," it said, "it is not your time. There is still so much work to be done." I began feeling overwhelmed with confusion, with the not-knowing. *What was the work I needed to do?*

I wanted direction, an explanation, the reasons why. Why did I have this experience? When these answers were not forthcoming, I became even more depressed. I felt sick, my life frozen, out of order. I felt unheard. I felt unseen.

Not once, but twice I'd seen and felt the "other side," the life after this life. I had witnessed the possibilities of the next life, with my own eyes. Awakening to the reality of my old life, I fought to shed my unhappiness, my inner fury, my rage, my gloom, unable to let go of the lingering dark energies that remained. I had to find the source of my pain and release it, so I could fully connect to Source.

It's a rare NDEr who doesn't suffer with some feelings of anger and depression. Being resuscitated, or brought back to life—perhaps against one's will—can leave some NDErs struggling to reconcile their experience, unable to accept or understand why they've been "sent back."

A spirit of discontent can infect even the most blissful NDE episode, and make this potential blessing seem like a burden.

In that state of mind, our friends and family can't help. Our everyday coping skills can't help. Sometimes even doctors, psychiatrists and therapy can't help.

I had tried it all. For years, I had been to doctors, therapists and psychiatrists. I'd sat on their leather couches, looked outside their windows, and talked. A lot. Even though I was being treated with medication, it didn't help; something dangerous was surging and building inside me.

Don't get me wrong—sharing my story in therapy helped, in the moment. Afterward, I felt a breath a fresh air rushing through me; yet I always found myself right back where I started, returning again and again to feeling desperate and disconnected, alone and lost.

I'd tried everything, and everything failed me. *Get me out of here!* my mind desperately pleaded, wanting to leave this world and be free of its torment. *Everyone will be better off, without me.*

The day the world would be better off without me, the day it would be okay if my Light diminished, was the same day I found a speck of the Light within me. That Light saved my life, when all was lost.

Depression is not a moment; it is an experience. You live with it, breathe with it, sleep with it. It was a haze that lingered with me throughout the day, a blanket of sadness and self-torture that kept me wrapped up tight. Sometimes the blanket was heavy, sometimes feather-light. Sometimes that blanket of sadness covered me completely; at other times, just a portion.

Yet my blanket wasn't just torture. It was a form of protection, too. People would give me space and leave me alone, cocooned inside my blanket.

My grandfather had schizophrenia; I was told it was because of the emotional stress in his life. In my unstable state, I became terrified that I'd develop the same mental illness. I was afraid that my extraordinary gifts were in fact a gifted imagination of mine, or the beginning of a rapidly-deteriorating mental disease. This was all the more reason not to talk about the paranormal gifts I was experiencing.

Defeating these distressing thoughts became impossible. At the same time, my mind was fighting to be free. Inside, I was desperate for change. Quietly, whenever I felt the grip of depression loosen, I opened my mind to the Light—and as I did, the gaping hole in my existence slowly filled. I was reminded that my identity was to be found in the Light, not in all the people I'd hurt, all the pain I'd caused. Holding back the tears, I realized, *I am who the Light says I am.* Suddenly I wanted to know what the Light saw that I didn't see, what the Light had planned for me.

And the transformation began.

OVERCOMING THE MONSTER OF DEPRESSION

The monster of depression can strike any one of us, at any time. Every day becomes a struggle, and we become locked in a ferocious, constant battle. Freeing ourselves from depression isn't easy—perhaps right now you feel like depression has control over you.

There is a way out. You may have to step into some uncomfortable territory. But just remember—overcoming discomfort builds empowerment, and frees you to live the life you were created to live, without the constant weight of depression.

1. Find Connection

Depression generates alienation. Alienation makes us want to hide, to isolate, to sneak away and live in a dark cave.

Don't isolate yourself. Find someone—a close friend or a place or a group to connect with. For NDErs, there are websites such as IANDS, or NDERF that offer information and support. Find an energy healer in your area and schedule an appointment. If needed, talk to your personal physician. I required medication after my NDE, but as I began studying LifeForce Energy Healing® I used those regenerative techniques to relieve and release my depression.

2. Engage with Nature

During my depression, I needed to escape the noise of life; I quickly learned that isolating myself was not helpful. Instead I turned to nature—I forced myself outside, and ran, or hiked, or took a walk. In nature, I found a quiet and peaceful connection with Spirit and my Soul. In nature, I opened myself up to the beauty and wonder of the universe, to the childlike awe of everything that surrounds us.

Connecting in nature was connecting with my guides, the angels and those in the Light. I found a language with Spirit in nature. My questions would be answered on a walk or a run, often without me even asking. This gave me great power and peace.

Engaging with nature helps us access a deep well of peace and serenity, and reduces anger, worry and stress. Get out from under the oppressive thumb of depression. Restore your mind by engaging with the transcendent beauty of nature.

3. Writing and Journaling

In the death-grip of depression, the daily exercise of journaling out my fear and my anger was a cathartic release. Finally, I had a *reason* to be afraid, to be angry, to cry! I discovered I was consumed by rage, yet also incredibly afraid. My anger and rage turned to fear—fear of failing everybody in my life, of never doing enough.

Purging these old emotions energized me. Motivated, I kept up with my journaling. Every time I would cry, I would journal about my fears. Each time, another fear was released. Each time, I healed a deeper part of me. Each time, I discovered a piece of me that was missing—soon I realized I was healing the holes I'd created in my energy field. With each journaling confession, each day, each hour, I was gaining awareness, strength and power.

I kept my journal close, at all times. In it, I confessed *everything*. I wrote down my feelings, noting who I was with, what I was doing, why I felt that way. I discovered an inner sadness I'd never identified. Jealousy, shame, guilt—all these emotions and more came pouring out of me. My venting became cathartic; it was necessary for me to know my emotions, my feelings, my anxieties, so I could own them. Knowing them allowed me to know myself.

The healing process involved confessing and declaring and communicating with myself. The act of journaling and writing was a necessary part of my journey. The stuff that came easily at first was just that—the beginning layer, the least challenging, least painful emotions to handle or get to. Soon, the other emotional walls came crumbling down—the walls I had been hiding behind, building a life on. Those forbidden tears would make their way again. As I wrote, as I journaled, I kept seeing myself as a young girl, hoping for and wanting validation, appreciation, love. I realized it was time I gave it to her.

I urge you to start a journal. Write some words, every day. Write to stay connected with yourself. Write to confess your sadness. Write to discover your happiness.

As you write, your words will become sentences that express your personal truths. Give your feelings a voice. Give your dreams encouragement. Expressing your dreams in writing is a powerful weapon against depression. Start today.

4. Healing through Meditation

For years I felt isolated, alone, disconnected from the world and everyone in it. I never believed that anyone would understand my feelings. I was disconnected from myself, from my friends and family, and from Spirit. It felt safer to disconnect. If I was disconnected, I didn't have to stand up for myself and say, *No.*

Meditation shifted my perspective. Meditation opened me to connection with something higher. My meditation teacher, Deborah King, had told her students, "Meditation is like a giant broom for sweeping away stagnant or blocked energy you have buried deep within your body." Hearing those words, my face lit up. I had stored so much pain. I could not name the pain, but it was there, overloading my brain, weighing me down like a ton of bricks. I knew I had to release whatever it was that was making me sick and tired and anxious.

Along with being sick and anxious, I had a mind that continually raced. Never did I believe I'd have the ability to slow down, to decelerate my life, and meditate. But I surrendered; I took the meditation course, received my mantra and followed the advice.

When I first meditated, I would shake periodically, or twitch. Closing my eyes, I'd see colors and blurry faces and bright lights. Other times, I saw nothing, felt nothing. I had no idea what kind of revelation or epiphany I expected—what *it* was I was waiting for—until *it* finally happened.

One day I awoke in meditation, in a place of pure love. I was surrounded in peace and light. Feeling my eyes tear up and my hands trembling, the tension lifting from my body, I smiled, finally experiencing the power and presence of Divine Love and energy—a place where *yes* or *no* never mattered, a place without panic attacks or stress. In this place I was shown images of my higher self, the person I was intended to be. Behind my closed and awestruck eyelids, it all became clear. There was a new life.

When I am stressed, angry or upset, I turn my mind to meditation. Meditation helps dissolve the energy that doesn't serve me. Meditation is my voice of encouragement, the voice that dares me to believe my best days are ahead of me. Without meditation, without that quiet place to go to, that place of clarity, hope and love, I would not be living my best life.

5. Find Your Joy

This might make you uncomfortable. This might trigger waves of panic. This might flood your mind with every counterintuitive fear, every negative doubt, every last desperate impulse to avoid it, reject it, instead of diving in head-first.

When I was locked in a battle with anxiety and PTSD, the usually-kind-and- sympathetic people in my life would say, "Take care of yourself! Do something that brings you *joy!*"

Joy?

Yes, *joy*. Yet joy was a sketchy concept to me. Joy was a word I did not associate with. I didn't know what joy was, other than to bring it to others. I'd mastered caring for others and knowing what would make *them* happy—yet I had no idea what brought *me* joy.

My heart was an empty space. I needed to make room, to release my fear and anger, for joy to fill the empty space.

Discovering what made *me* happy was a challenge. What did I like to do? What truly made me feel good? What filled me up with enough joy for myself that I could share the joy with others?

I had been lost for so long from myself, I barely knew. Like a brain-injured trauma patient, I needed to re-learn from the very beginning how to walk, how to talk, how to stand, how to sit. I needed to return to the basics, and find the pieces of me I'd lost along the way.

I did the work. I went back to childhood. As a child, I'd been rewarded with love and attention when I was good, and affirmation and approval when I did good. Was it a Catholic thing? Maybe. Regardless of how it had originally formed, I'd found my love of self in giving to others—the problem was, that's not how it was intended for us to live, experiencing life only through others. I have my journey, and you have yours. It's not my place nor my purpose to make your journey so right, so perfect, so pleasant and blessed and yet forget mine all the way.

If I wanted peace, if I craved purpose, I needed to *find joy*.

So it began: The next step in my journey. I had set the intent, emptied my heart, and released the anger. My hands shook as I prepared for the next phase, the next stage. Now it was time for joy.

Uncertain where I would find it, I set aside free time for myself, and waited. I couldn't think of anything to do. Being alone, just me, was hard.

I had no idea where to begin. Nothing that would possibly bring me joy crossed my mind. The sheer effort of it was exhausting.

Finally, I found myself going back to my old ways, deciding to volunteer at a home for the aging and dying Sister Servants of the Immaculate Heart of Mary—but this time, I went into it differently. Instead of being assigned a place and a job, I advised them what I might be good at, and when I'd be available. It felt good to walk through the doors and be greeted with kind smiles and warm eyes. I felt the connection with Mary, and I enjoyed being in her presence.

Soaking in the love of Mary, I found joy. I found joy in prayer and connection with Spirit—it was not about the nuns or the church or the work I did there. It was learning to find joy in Spirit. This wasn't an experience I'd allowed myself to entertain, yet in shock I was finding joy in everything. I found joy in silence; in my nature walks; in moments of writing. I found joy in the sound of the rain. I even found joy in the *nothing*—in just *being*. I realized joy was in the act of self-discovery.

Finding your joy is a process of digging—taking the time to get to know your emotions and feelings, your deepest desires and dreams, and then aligning them with the rest of your life.

Here's what I found. Not only did my connection to Spirit and Mary and all that exists bring me joy, but I began to understand that Spirit was directing me to experience and uncover *more* joy, more dreams, more desires, more potential pathways to walk in the Light, bringing more of me *into* me.

Slowly but surely, this opened up a whole world of understanding about myself. The struggle to know myself lessened. The puzzle of finding myself was beginning to take shape, pieces to an enormous puzzle clicking into place. That alone brought me joy.

Suddenly my heart wanted to explode with joy. The constant ache to feel fulfilled was gone, replaced by the purest manifestation of self-love. I kept a journal of my joyful feelings, and the lingering questions that zigzagged through my mind. I had to get to know how and why I felt; I had to learn the lessons of myself, so that I could teach myself how to *be me.*

The journey to finding joy never ends.

One day, without warning, a young woman poked her head into my office. "Cathy Gabrielsen? I'm your two o'clock appointment," she said.

Silently she strode in, her head down. I knew this young woman was depressed when she entered; she was wearing grey sweatpants and a sweat-shirt. She was young, just a sophomore in college; a formerly vibrant and bright-eyed superstar athlete at her school, heading off to study medicine at a university away from her hometown.

Yet her energy felt slow, lethargic, and I could feel the sadness. *She's trying to perc herself up,* I told myself. Openly she began to share with me stories about the sickness in her family, how the ongoing care her beloved grandmother required was a stress on her parents. She was especially close with her grandmother—she'd been present when her grandmother took her last breath. She also shared with me the story of her recent romantic breakup, the challenges of her relationships at school, and her inability to trust people, especially the other girls. They made up stories about her and her sexual activity, and spread rumors.

As I sat there listening to her release what she had been longing to share, I experienced sharp pains in my body, especially my second and third chakras. My chest tightened, stabbing me with panic—I knew it wasn't mine, it was hers. I was just picking up on her energy field and her emotions.

What I heard from this girl's heart was a deep unhappiness about where she was; she wasn't sure she wanted to be in medicine after all. She doubted she would make a good physician as she'd been unable to emotionally handle the death of her grandmother. I felt her heart ache and my throat began to close and tingle, letting me know that she was not speaking her truth.

I wasn't surprised then when she confessed she'd started cutting herself. The thought of suicide had also come up, twice recently. As she told me, she cried. How much I identified with her, in that moment! She was scared she would let people down—her parents especially. She was scared to tell anyone at school, the same people who bullied her and spread rumors. She was afraid what they would say about her, how they'd use her truth to mock and ridicule her.

When I perform my healing work, I connect with a higher source of energy, a source of the Light. I stand as a witness, my body becoming a conduit of restorative light. I work with Divine Female energy; at times I've felt the presence of St. Theresa of Avila. When I see her, she enters carrying a single gift: A rose.

That day, sitting next to this young woman and asking quietly in the silence of my heart for help, I began to hear the word, *Teresa…Teresa.* Confused, I asked my client her middle name, expecting her to say the word Teresa—instead, she answered, "Rose." Chills ran through my body; instantly I experienced the presence of St. Teresa. I felt my client's sadness release, the darkness leave her, like smoke rising in a flame. I knew Teresa was working on my client's heart, and saw her filling it with pink rose petals.

The next day, I received a text from this young woman, telling me how amazing she felt. She'd made the tough decision to tell her parents, her friends and family that she was going to do what she wanted to do with her life, to go where she wanted to go, to study what she wanted to study (not medicine). She felt much better, she told me. For the first time in a long time, she said, she felt joy.

I believe the day each of us stops fighting our dreams and learns to trust in them and honor them is the day we begin to find true joy, and become a benefit to others. Waking up to joy unleashes your passion, instead of keeping it asleep. Waking to your dreams forces you to come out of your lulled state of disconnection, of discouragement, of depression. Finding the joy in your heart will clear your head and your heart, and set you free.

Are you sinking in despair? Are you lost and afloat in the raging waters of depression? Muster your courage, trigger your dreams, and wake out of the darkness, by exploring what it means to find connection, to engage in nature, to experience peace through meditation, and to find lasting joy.

Find joy by being contemplative. Find joy by connecting with your feelings. Find joy by being truthful to yourself. When we find what brings us joy, we find *ourselves*.

Finding ourselves is one of the most powerful weapons in fighting depression. In the pages that follow, I'll show you how to use that same life-changing joy in blocking out and overriding the negative noise of one of the most debilitating issues that face each of us—anxiety.

9

Anxiety After an NDE

FEAR RAN THROUGH MY LIMBS, MY HEAD, MY STOMACH. Fear rushed through my veins and moved swiftly into my bloodstream, surging up from my heart to my throat, taking over my airway. My breaths became shallow and short. *Breathe, Cathy, breathe!* I begged myself. But my breaths felt more like an exhale then an inhale. When I breathed in, little air pulsed into my lungs. I felt like I was drowning, but I was still above the water, waiting to dive into the pool with the rest of my swim team.

That was my first panic attack. The first time I remember experiencing a battle with anxiety.

They say the first person to hear about your NDE plays an important role in your integration process.

I had no one to talk to after my first NDE. I'd been hurled into chaos— my boyfriend in a coma with a traumatic brain injury, on the brink of death, injured in a horrific car accident from which I'd somehow survived. My *story,* my *near-death experience,* felt insignificant at the time, so I never shared it. I buried it. I buried the questions and the possibilities. There was so much I wanted to talk about, so much I wanted to confess, but never did. I believed no one would understand. This was not the time to focus on me or my issues, my pain, my concerns—it was a time to focus on Tom.

Hopefully the time for me to share, to heal from my trauma would come. But days passed. Months passed. And then years passed. I never took the opportunity to share what had happened to me in Tom's car, what it was like to nearly die. I was afraid of my truth, so I never spoke of it.

Never speaking out about the accident, my terror, my near-death, my guilt at surviving the crash while my boyfriend Tom lingered at death's doorway—all that fueled a firestorm of angst and physical distress, beating my body into painful submission. All that angst and distress had nowhere to go, nowhere to be released, except into my overwhelmed mind.

All the angst and distress created anxiety.

Having no release, no way out, anxiety devoured me. Anxiety gnawed at me, and consumed my thoughts, leaving me imprisoned in a glazed silence. Anxiety was my voice that needed speaking, my heart that needed love and mending, my soul that longed to live and soar. Anxiety was the fear of letting everyone down, the guilt of wanting to leave Tom and move on with my life, the shame of even thinking that thought at all.

My anxiety also came from the uncertainty, the unpredictability of my emotional state. My anxiety was always talking to me, whispering to me, telling me no one would ever understand, no one would believe, everyone I told would mock me, ridicule me, hate me.

Anxiety wasn't just winning—anxiety had already won. Anxiety took control of my mind, incarcerating me in a cage of confusion, apprehension and shock. Anxiety kept me from understanding myself or my NDE, a shadow that never seemed to leave me—I was a prisoner in the dark, blind to what I couldn't grasp, mind deep in stress, and locked in a constant battle to comprehend what had happened to me.

anx·i·e·ty (aNGˈzīədē)

1. A nervous disorder characterized by a state of excessive uneasiness and apprehension, typically with compulsive behavior or panic attacks.

Anxiety is usually triggered by a build-up of stressful life situations—a death in the family, brooding about work, worry over finances. It's a common mental state that even normal, everyday people face.

NDErs suffering anxiety feel even more anxious, more fearful, more distressed and agitated than normal people—because they don't feel "normal."

Normal people suffering an NDE have a difficult time feeling "normal" because so much has changed. Many NDEr's discover unwanted intuitive abilities, or develop a deeper, more sensitive side—at times, painfully-sensitive, and over-reactive.

My anxiety always came on quickly, suddenly—it felt like a heart attack. I pictured myself trapped on a sinking ship, and needed to get everyone out. Closing my eyes, I'd try to calm my breath, breathing slowly in and out, while the warm sensation of blood pulsed in my chest and chills crept up my spine. Beginning in my heart area and across the back of my shoulders, everything tightened and constricted. To fight the feeling I'd begin to stretch my shoulders back, trying to open my heart. Sensing an attack, I'd announce to my husband, "Here it comes," then pop an Ativan and wait for the attack to pass.

My anxiety reared its head because I was feeling all these new things about myself, but I could not share them. I was confused about myself and what I was feeling. After the car accident, I felt like I was hearing directions—where to place my hands on Tom, what to do to help him. Immediately following the event the *knowing*, the *guidance* kept coming, unwanted, unasked for, unannounced. Distressed by this, I began talking quietly to myself, engaged in a battle in my head, telling myself, *I must be going crazy.*

Instead of my NDE and the Light I'd encountered bringing me peace, bringing me comfort, it created intense confusion, panic, and inner torment. Instead of being connected by the Light, I felt ostracized by my experience. Instead of my NDE becoming my liberator, it became my predator.

Instead of becoming the person the Light pronounced me to be, I became more insecure, more deeply ensnared in a quagmire of self-doubt, more battered by a barrage of destructive thoughts than ever.

I *became* the anxiety.

When I asked my husband, "What was my worst battle with anxiety?" he replied it was at the beach, right before I decided to get well.

Only vaguely do I remember it; when you are in a state of anxiety, time stops, and you leave your body. I left my body a lot back then. We were staying in a beach town called Avalon that summer. I knew when I walked the beach in those days, alone with my thoughts, that there was something shifting in me. I was still taking lots of medication, to help overcome my emotional issues. One night, I overheard someone telling my husband I was over-medicated. It was a tipping point.

Over-medicated? I thought. *Me?* Suddenly a jolt of panic burst through me; my old battle with perfectionism was triggered. I was supposed to be the one everyone said positive things about. I was so nice and sweet and kind. I had the big heart; I had done such great things for the community. Yet here, in this beach town, someone saw me negatively, not as the perfect person I had worked so hard to be. It was crushing; in an instant, my world began falling apart. The expectation I had for myself became much too heavy for me to carry. I was collapsing under my own pressure, afraid that if I failed to be perfect, people would no longer accept me, love me.

Now, as I walked the beach, tormenting thoughts popped up like mushrooms. I had created it all: I set up the expectations, expectations that I would do everything and be everything to everyone. I would gladly sacrifice myself for others, because I related that sacrifice to love. Suddenly, I was enraged; squinting around the beach at everyone, I thought, *I'm okay with not being loved anymore.*

My husband says I cried all afternoon at the beach. He came to check on me as I sat in the same chair in the same spot for hour upon hour, contemplating. Wondering who else thought I was over-medicated, who else thought I was addicted, who no longer thought I was the perfect version of myself.

The gig was up. People saw my flaws; they saw me as vulnerable and imperfect.

I knew I was over-medicated—but I knew I needed help. And soon after, I found the help I needed.

In a sense, I was in a state of withdrawal from the Light. Whenever the Light left my system, fear came flooding back.

Fear can become our truth. My fears became mine. I lived in fear of people knowing the real me. I was terrified the real me would disappoint others, so I modeled and molded myself into the expectation everyone desired. In every situation, I mastered their need, their want of me.

And I became it.

At home, I was the perfect child. I listened; I did everything my parents asked. I was quiet, never rebellious or acting out. I was all my church taught us to be—respectful, mindful, loving, kind, selfless, giving, serving and spiritual. I followed all the rules of our home, our school and our religion. I became *perfect,* in their eyes.

The more I followed the rules, the better accepted I was. So I kept doing exactly as I was told. It felt so safe to follow direction—it was easier, the decisions were made for me, and there would be no feathers ruffled.

I was a perfect follower.

Writing became one way out of anxiety—I started a diary. In the process of writing I learned my thoughts were my fears. Every time I feared being imperfect or letting someone down, I'd immediately become anxious. Over-doing and over-being, I became just what everyone wanted me to be—but not *me.*

Acknowledging my fear of imperfection, knowing my fear of letting people down was one thing. Letting the fears go—that was something entirely different. It took trying and failing and failing and trying to learn how to let go of the fear.

The problem was the fears ran so deep. I needed to dig deeper, into my past, to finally let it all go.

I pictured my first panic attack. I was 8 years old, standing on the diving platform in the early morning, getting ready to dive into the early summer pool water. Swim team meets had begun. As a child, I'd played many team sports—my dad had served as my coach, and the family photographer, never missing an opportunity to watch me play. My mom was rarely able to attend any afterschool events—she was busy working outside the home while raising 5 children. On this day, as usual, my father was there. And on this day, the coach asked me to swim two laps. She had faith in me and my abilities—it was myself who lacked faith. Not yet mastering the flip-turn, I would need to reach out and touch the wall, then kick off. I was afraid of not looking good, fearful the wall touch would slow me down, that I would lose time and finish last in my heat. I was nervous—but I became petrified, when I looked up and saw my mom enter the meet.

Panic raced through my body, pounding my brain. Don't get me wrong—I was ecstatic she was there. I loved my mom so much, and desperately wanted her to be proud of me. *Don't mess this up, Cathy!* I pleaded with myself. My breaths became shallow. Taking my place on the diving board, I felt sick to my stomach, and my vision fogged, everything turning blurry. Sounds rattled my head, every noise becoming more intense, more dramatic. Everyone and everything seemed to move faster than I did—I was moving, seeing and breathing in slow-motion.

Hearing the whistle, then the pop of the air gun, the race began. I was last in the pool. Seconds into the race, it felt as though my lungs had filled with water. *I'm drowning!* my panicked mind screamed. I pulled myself to the side of the pool, hopped out, and in disgust I walked away.

I don't remember much else from that day. I don't remember searching people's eyes as I nearly crawled to the dressing room, my stomach churning. I don't remember anyone asking if I was okay, if I was alright. It didn't matter; I'd let them all down. I'd let my mother down, and failed.

That miserable experience had nearly been forgotten—until I was searching for myself, my fears and ways to release the anxiety from my body. Recalling it, and re-experiencing the pain, I vowed to do something different.

I decided to start speaking to myself, as if I were that 8-year-old child. I realized I was that perfect child. For decades, both of us had been locked together in a prison cell of unworthiness. *Today we're coming out of that cell,* I told her, and in my mind I held out my arms to hug her. I'd found her on my journey, and where I would go from that moment onward, I would take her.

Before I could bring her with me, though, I had to remove the fear.

I closed my eyes, and imagined the two of us—me as a child and me as an adult, standing on the edge of the pool. This time however, there would be someone to tell her it was okay, that she was safe, she wasn't drowning and there was nothing to be afraid of. Looking down at her face, I saw her pleading eyes, her broken heart and her shaky body, and I calmed her, I loved her, and comforted her. I brought the little girl with me, carrying her and walking alongside her, hand-in-hand, as we marched together away from the pool, on the road of this new healing journey.

Fear was no longer my truth. As I embraced my real truth, my anxiety fell by the wayside. As I shed more and more anxiety, I exposed the lies and was liberated from them, overcoming the falsehoods of insecurity with my own truth.

HEALING ANXIETY

But maybe you're not there yet. Most of us have to learn to attack anxiety by taking small steps. We learn to overcome and heal from anxiety by going through a series of stages.

Anxiety keeps us locked in a lie—that life has thrown us into a trap, and there's no escape. The only way to break free of the trap is to take the first step. It's the fear of actually stepping out of the trap that paralyzes us.

Take a moment to consider each of these healing first steps, then boldly step into action.

1. Self-Awareness

Taking the time to learn about myself and my emotions was critical to my healing. I needed to know what *it* was that was causing me anxiety. I needed to discover the fear, so I could let it go from my body.

One day, I sketched a stick figure on a piece of paper. At the bottom, the foot of the stick figure, I wrote down the first fear I could recall. As my pencil moved up the body of the stick figure, I wrote the next fear; then the next, and the next, until I reached the top. Looking at the fears I'd sketched, I discovered they had a common thread: That I was afraid not to do good, not to be good, not to speak good, to fail and to let someone down. Doing those things meant I was not lovable.

The self-awareness, the recognition I felt was shocking. Suddenly I understood why I did things, why I felt things. From that moment on, I was able to stop and ask myself: *Why am I doing this? For love? For recognition? For fear of letting someone down?*

Realizing my choices were for the wrong reasons transformed me—I found the power to say *No*. It was permissible, even noble, to say *No*. Saying *No* when I needed silenced the guilt and the negative voices resounding in my mind, voices that kept me from hearing the positive voice of the Light.

Self-awareness takes time. Take the time to know yourself. Dig under the lies you've assumed about yourself, the lies others have poisoned you with, and discern the truth. Then align with that truth. In doing so, you'll find yourself; in finding yourself, you'll find peace.

Finding Me: An Exercise in Self Awareness:

1. In this exercise, we're going to meet our inner self, our inner child, our perfect self. For this exercise to be of value, you must open yourself fully, allowing yourself to imagine what you were like as a child. Take a breath in through your nose, and exhale through your mouth. Repeat this a few times.

2. Dismiss any distractions or errant thoughts in your mind. Send this unbending intent to your heart: *I need to be found.* Finding *you* is as important as searching for a missing child. With your eyes closed, tell yourself, *I am coming to find you.*

3. In the quiet of your body, listen to your blood flowing. Listen to your heart beating. Listen in silence. Ask your Spirit again: *Show me. Where am I? I need to be found.*

4. The first answer you hear is where *you* are resting. Go there. Go to wherever you hear you are with compassion, with love. Go to yourself.

5. See yourself. What are you doing? Are you standing? Sitting? How do you feel? What do you need? Observe yourself.

6. Before you say anything, return to your physical self. Hug yourself. Look at your pure and perfect self. Tell yourself: *You are loved. And I'm so glad I found you.*

7. Take this moment in silence. Listen to the conversation. Just *be* with yourself; words are not necessary as much as the feeling of love and compassion. Intend that you are sending this love and compassion to yourself.

8. Finally, go to your heart. See yourself, standing tall, holding hands, surrounded in white light. The light is washing over you like a waterfall, purifying you, cleansing and releasing the pain from the past. Continue holding hands, together, breathing in and out.

9. Slowly open your eyes. You have connected with yourself. Congratulations! This is the first step in healing.

Things to Remember:

- Self-knowledge is the most powerful element to personal happiness and fulfillment. Take the time, start learning, start uncovering the keys to self-knowledge; discover ways to really know yourself.

- Self-awareness creates self-control. You cannot control yourself until you *know yourself.*

- Identifying and acknowledging your emotions creates self-awareness. Keep a notebook, a journal, a diary. Write down each feeling. Keep a list. Discover how you feel, and why.

In all my years of helping people overcome anxiety, no one has ever said to me, "You know, Cathy, becoming more self-aware was a bad decision. I wish I'd never taken that step." The missing puzzle pieces to our life start to show up, as we become more self-aware. But becoming self-aware doesn't mean we don't need others to help us heal. Quite the opposite.

2. Find a Tribe

Surround yourself with those who appreciate you, your story, your positive side and your flaws, without judgment or criticism. Surround yourself with a tribe of people whose presence sustains you, uplifts you, inspires you, whose presence makes you vibrate at a higher level.

Tribe with those who are in the Light. Find yourself a healing circle or a prayer circle. Meet with your circle several times a month. Fill yourself with the energy of your circle. Fill others with your own passion and affirmation.

Surrounding yourself with a tribe of open-minded, compassionate souls will lead you and motivate you and lift your spirit. Surrounding yourself with negative, fear-based souls will have you experiencing the same—you'll become negative, anxious, narrow-minded, wandering in the dark. You can easily find a tribe on Facebook by searching the keywords *anxiety, healing, PTSD, NDE,* or *healing circles.* Google the words, and connect with your tribe.

3. Movement

When I was trapped in anxiety, paralyzed by fear, the safest place to be was at home. Home was my comfort zone. Home was my shelter, comfortable and quiet. I could close the blinds, lock the doors, and keep life out.

But keeping life locked outside actually caused the anxiety to grow and thrive. As I confined myself, the negative energy gained more power. What I needed to do was simple—*move!* I needed get into action, get moving, do something that got my energy field flowing.

Managing anxiety is like managing pain. When managing pain, the best advice is to "get to the pain *before* the pain gets to you." When you feel an attack of anxiety, immediately launch a counter-attack of action, of movement. Take a walk in nature; practice yoga; go fishing; play tennis; ride a bike—whatever it is, find a way to *move.* The goal is to move the negative energy out of your field.

I began by taking long walks in my neighborhood, intending to connect with nature. I wanted to get out of my head and into the natural world around me. The walks felt good; they became a routine that made me feel safe and linked to my surroundings. Whenever I found myself experiencing the tightening in my chest, the first signs of an anxiety attack, instead of heading to a quiet room and locking myself in, I laced up my shoes and headed out for my walk. And guess what? By moving, by attacking my anxiety first, the attack of anxiety never came.

4. Clear Your Chakras

Get to know your personal energy field—your chakras. Clear, balance and recharge your field every day.

My first experience with a healer was after being diagnosed with cancer. I had no idea what I was getting myself into, but knew I needed healing. Immediately the healer went to work on my heart chakra. As she did, thoughts swirled in my head—at the time I had no clue what a *chakra* was all about.

She began by focusing my attention on every part of my body, asking me what each part felt like. I forced myself to focus; it was the first time I'd concentrated on my body, honored my body. I honored my feet, my ankles, my ears. I honored every limb, every organ. I developed an acute awareness of my body, the capsule of my soul, an awareness I had never known. I had to know me to feel me, to heal me.

That afternoon I felt my body's energy rise to the surface. The energy unwound and released, liberating a flow of peace. I sensed the power of my own energy, my own field working in a way I hadn't known. It was *my* personal energy field, *my* body, *my* power.

It would be years and many other diseases later before I began a daily practice of clearing, balancing and recharging my chakras. A daily practice of connecting with your body, your energy field, and releasing the negative energy, the negative emotions, heals anxiety. I am the healthiest, the happiest and most fulfilled I have ever been, thanks to opening myself to the healing power and possibilities of energy medicine.

5. Find the Root of Fear

Months after my NDE, after facing the devastating fear of death, after being locked in cycles of crushing anxiety, depression and PTSD, I desperately wanted change. I'd ask people, "What is *wrong* with me?" They didn't know; they couldn't help. Disheartened, fear drove me to the brink of considering suicide.

Under the impulses of panic and anxiety, I reached the bottom of my fears. There I realized: *I need to find out what I'm afraid of.* Where was the fear? Where had it come from?

Taking out my journal, I scribbled down everything I was afraid of. Line after line of fears: Losing my mind, losing my children, getting another disease, getting fat. Fear after fear I wrote. What I discovered was this: They were all rooted in the same thing.

I was afraid I wouldn't be there for someone who needed me. I was afraid of hurting someone, and being unable to save them.

This clarified everything. Seeing each fear for what it was, I was able to accept that fear, acknowledge that fear, then let each fear go. *Goodbye, fear of getting a disease! Goodbye, fear of getting fat!* At the root of my fears I found an unexpected emotion—anger. A raging anger had been planted underneath each fear, creating a toxic buildup of endless distress.

My anger shocked me. After a few days of rooting further down and discovering my fears, I performed the same exercise with anger. This was difficult; I had never identified myself as an angry person. *What am I so angry about?* I dug deeper into my psyche, uncovering simple things like, *I was angry for forgetting my wallet at checkout that day.* As soon as I opened the door, as soon as I allowed the thought of anger to step inside, I began unleashing episode after episode I was angry about.

At my core was my anger about being unloved. No one was interested in helping me; nobody had my back or cared about me. Everyone took advantage of my good nature and my loving, caring, giving spirit. Those thoughts unleashed more anger—and then just like that, the anger came and came. And then, it evaporated. It was gone.

Anger, fear, guilt and shame—these dark energies were weighing me down, and I didn't even know it. They disrupted the energy flow in my lower chakras. Their overwhelming presence created an opening and room for more dark energies to flood in—that dark energy wanted *more*. My life was overflowing with heavy emotions, raging fire and heat that needed the water of my tears to be extinguished.

Journaling out my fear and anger was a cathartic release. I had been living most of my life in a *fight or flight* response. I was exhausting my adrenals and drowning in fearful anxiety. I kept up with my journaling, digging for more roots. Each time I found one, I released it. Each time I released a fear, I healed a part of me that needed healing. Each time, I was gaining awareness, inner strength and power.

These are some of the ways I was able to defeat my fears, my anxiety, and heal myself. Yet my battles with anxiety after my NDE were only part of a bigger battle, a battle that kept returning me to the moments during Tom's accident when I felt terrorized by irrational panic, a panic that proclaimed its existence with each painful stab in my brain, a panic that didn't stop coming until decades later, when I began my war against an even bigger monster—the demon of PTSD.

10

PTSD After an NDE

WHAT IS PTSD?

What does a PTSD attack feel like?

A pounding heartbeat. Difficulty breathing. Dizziness, shaking, trembling. Stomach pain. Nausea. Uncontrolled mood swings. Depressive highs. Manic lows.

These are a few of the symptoms of post-traumatic stress disorder, commonly referred to as PTSD.

PTSD is triggered by some terrifying event in one's life—either experiencing it or witnessing it. Most of us upon hearing the term immediately think of war veterans, firefighters or police officers—those who've served on a battlefield, whether in the heat of war or on our own neighborhood streets. Years ago, it was referred to as "shell shock" or "combat fatigue." Nowadays, PTSD is found all around us, in survivors of all types of trauma.

According to statistics, PTSD affects 3.5% of American adults. The symptoms show a wide range of severity—from fearful, intrusive thoughts, flashbacks or nightmares to chronic feelings of numbness, estrangement, irritability. Feeling lightheaded or sick to your stomach can also be a symptom of PTSD.

Most people who go through traumatic events like an NDE may have temporary difficulty adjusting and coping—yet over time, their coping skills can improve. If symptoms linger or worsen, interfering with your daily functioning, you may have PTSD.

PTSD symptoms after experiencing a near-death episode can include the following:

- Recurring, traumatic memories of the event
- Reliving the NDE as if it were happening again (flashbacks)
- Unsettling dreams about your NDE
- Severe anguish or anxiety to something that reminds you of the NDE
- An avoidance of thinking or speaking about the episode
- Avoiding places or people who remind you of the episode
- Negative changes in mood, in thoughts about yourself
- Apathy or hopelessness about your future
- Memory issues; being unable to recall the event
- Trouble sleeping or concentrating
- Feeling the need to remain on-guard for constant danger

The first time I experienced PTSD was in the aftermath of Tom's car accident; the second was after my bout with sepsis, when I'd developed a serious bacterial infection. I was never quite sure what it was that invaded my body and my blood and wreaked havoc on my system. Afterward, I became terrified of becoming sick, of catching any germ that might develop into a life-threatening illness. Constantly I found myself asking everyone around if *they* were okay. Did they have a cold? A virus? Even going to the supermarket made me tremble with dread. I did everything to avoid being around sick people, and carried hand sanitizer with me at all times. I was obsessed with germs, viruses, and bugs to a fanatic intensity.

I also experienced PTSD upon the sudden re-removal of my breast. That was a significant trauma, and I was deeply traumatized by the surgery. There was a possibility that the germ was the result of a breast surgery I'd had a month prior to being in sepsis. I was having complications due to an implant and scar tissue, so they performed a minor surgery to remove the painful tissue around my implant. It is likely that a germ of some sort entered my breast or the implant during that time. Thinking about this became my new obsession, my worst nightmare.

My downward path with PTSD continued. About five years after sepsis, I needed surgery to repair some surgical mesh that was related to my breast reconstruction. At that time, my PTSD came roaring back out of nowhere—it had been years since my sepsis battle, yet surgery had triggered the sepsis before, and I became convinced that I'd receive another infection and go into sepsis. Emotionally out-of-control, fear exploded in my brain, escalating into a full-blown panic attack, as I re-experienced the original trauma.

Hitting rock bottom, I replayed the incident over and over in my mind. I became a prisoner inside our house. I planned nothing, expecting that I would be back in the hospital with a complication any day. During my worst moments, I'd hide myself in the family room on the couch, or lock myself in our bedroom. Unknowingly, I was in active PTSD when I came across Deborah King's website. It was during this time, after talking with my psychiatrist, that I was formally diagnosed with PTSD, and began therapy to deal with it.

Post-traumatic stress after an NDE can be especially traumatic.

I had no idea what PTSD was, though I'd lived with it for years after my car accident. The act of nearly dying was terrifying—I experienced tormenting nightmares from the accident, waking me in a panic that continued throughout the day. On and off I replayed the terror—the visions of the mud, the blood, the broken and wrecked car. The memory of my illness, the sudden loss of my breast, created another layer of panic and anxiety, worry and fear. The PTSD came from nearly dying, and then having to live.

PTSD can be easily triggered—in my case, I would hear a car crash on TV and relive the horror of Tom's accident. For survivors of NDEs, sights, sounds and even smells similar to those they experienced during the event can be PTSD triggers. Common triggers remind NDErs of the circumstances of their near-death—whether pleasant or disturbing, blissful or traumatic.

My triggers included winding, curving country roads, rain, or any kind of poor visibility while driving—probably because in the moments right before Tom's crash we failed to see the oncoming ravine. Driving winding rural roads after the accident, I'd become gripped by terror, intense waves of fear washing over me, believing the car was about to spin off the road and crash. Seeing brake lights, I'd sometimes scream or cry out "Slow down!" I was triggered by any talk about germs, any discussion of illness. Imagining I might need another surgery, I could again be triggered.

Still to this day, my mind remains on alert, easily triggered. I recognize the triggers when they appear, and I honor them, I understand them and I do my best to soothe them. I am no longer affected by PTSD; yet my body remembers the trauma, an experience no amount of time can ever wash away.

Post-traumatic stress is common for those who've survived an NDE—we suffered a terrifying incident, a trauma that nearly killed us. I struggled to function in the world after my NDE. I felt I was living in an altered reality—unfortunately it was my new reality, one that no one would understand. When I was in full-blown PTSD, trembling and quivering with anxiety, no one could comfort me. The fear would rise to the surface, monopolize every fiber of my being, until it had enough of me.

Always I was consumed by the terror of *not knowing*—not knowing when the terrible feelings of replaying the accident would rise and devour me; not knowing how long they would last; not knowing when they would return; not even knowing why I had come back to life in the first place. *Why wasn't I good enough die, to live in the Light?*

Struggling with PTSD, I struggled with trying to manage and comprehend the reason I still existed. After my NDE, I lost the fear of death.

But I became fearful of life.

Life terrified me. I knew I was different, that I needed to find a way to live in the chaos of my mind, my spirit, my body. I'd become different from my family and friends because of my experience, and the information I'd been shown about life after death, information they would never believe or understand.

In those moments in the Light, I realized there was a destiny, a purpose for my life. I formed an unbending intent to discover my soul's purpose.

One conclusion was in my head, one conclusion I would carry throughout my journey. *My NDEs saved my life. My NDEs can save me from my PTSD.* I knew I had to do something to heal, and that "something" was all in my hands.

HEALING FROM PTSD

There are many successful methods of using the gift of your NDE, to heal from post-traumatic stress.

1. Journal Your PTSD

I've mentioned the power of writing before. When I experienced an attack of PTSD, I went to my journal, writing down everything I felt. I needed to introduce myself to my PTSD feelings. Once I saw them on paper, I became aware of them. In the awareness, they could be released.

2. Reclaim Your Power

When I was in PTSD, I felt powerless. It was important for me to reclaim my personal power. How? Do something different! Power up your third chakra, and do something you've never done before. Take dance lessons, or singing lessons. Go on a hike, learn to paint, or take in a movie alone. Try a new sport, a new hobby. Set a goal for yourself, whether it's to run a race or paint a room—do something you've never done before, and take back turf from the enemy.

3. Create Moments of Joy

In the previous chapter, I urged you to *find* your joy. Now that you've found your joy, you can *create* moments of joy. Have fun! Put music on that makes you feel good. Sing and dance. Enjoy your coffee, your tea, your favorite hobby, your new book. Set aside time every day and fill it with something joyful. Joy strengthens our inner resilience against every obstacle, helping us overcome anything life can throw at us.

4. Meditate

Silencing the mind twice a day in meditation heals all levels of pain. Mantra-based meditation restored my energy field, healed my body, expanded my awareness and lifted my consciousness. The gift of my time in meditation was learning I didn't need to die to live—that in the silence, I could feel the unconditional love, the divine Light, and connect with all that is.

5. Let Go of Control

Every negative thought, event or emotion in your life can be defeated by the simple act of letting go of control.

I was once asked to speak before a group of young women. When I speak in public, the majority of what I say is guided by Spirit, much like my hands-on energy work.

On one occasion, before I was to present, someone had asked for a copy of the speech I was to give. Connecting with my guides, I wrote up a document. Soon after I sent it, I received word that the person overseeing the event wanted me to speak on specific topics—*on this, and that,* to *use these words and those words.* Quickly I realized my choice of words in the document spoke often about Spirit, and Source, and Energy Healing. I paused, taking the time to discern her request; I have a difficult time speaking another person's words.

The request felt very uncomfortable for me; I knew the energy I felt was that of *control.* I needed to understand and discern whose control it was. Was this *my* need for control, or the other woman's? Maybe it was a bit of both. I formatted a new and shorter presentation, allowing me to speak my truth, my words, creating a separate section for them to speak theirs.

The negative energy I'd sensed struck an uncomfortable cord with me. What lay under the need for control and power over the situation was fear. It was not my job to discern her fear. My job was to look with the eyes of compassion and know she was simply afraid.

Ironically, that same day I ran into a soon-to-be client's mother. She approached me, wanting to share a backstory as to why her daughter needed my help. Politely I interrupted her. "I'd rather hear the backstory from your daughter," I said—yet she continued sharing the daughter's story, offering suggestions and advice on the best way I could heal her.

For this woman, it was all about *control.* She was trying to control my words, my guidance, my healing. Instantly I knew she controlled all aspects in her life, as well as the lives of those close to her—because she could, and because she needed to. Control was the cornerstone of her survival as an adult, and probably as a child. Controlling the situation was all she knew, all she had ever known. Control was safe for her; it was her greatest defense mechanism. Lack of control terrified her.

After the experiences with these two women, I knew there was a message for me. These experiences were meant to teach me something. I asked myself, *Where was my need for control, in all of this?*

I had spent the majority of this lifetime in silence, never speaking my truth. I was afraid that my truth, my values, my ideas, my core beliefs and the essence of me, would not be what was expected, appreciated, accepted or liked. So I remained silent. I had once believed that my silence would be bliss. But I was wrong.

My truth was not in silence. Silence became *my control.* My truth was to let go of control, surrender to the Light and know me, to be the best version of me. My truth was to understand that when I feel the energy of control and power coming at me, I will view it from a higher perspective, and be empowered with the energy of kindness and compassion. My power is in my understanding that love and compassion will always overcome the energy of fear.

If you let go of control, you can be free.

6. Take Charge of Your Thoughts

Your thoughts become your reality, plain and simple. The key to overcoming PTSD or anxiety or any thought that is taking control of your mind is to know you have a way out—but that you won't win the war in your mind without a fight.

Overcoming your negative thought-processes will incite revolutionary change in your life. Taking charge of your thoughts is a stick of dynamite that can explode your self-destructive fears and behavior.

Let me share an example.

My husband and my two teenage sons are addicted to the TV series *Game of Thrones.* It is not my choice of entertainment; I pride myself on protecting myself and my energy field, keeping my experiences to the positive as much as humanly possible.

One night, as I was in our kitchen, the rest of the family was watching *Game of Thrones.* The sound of a young girl screaming, sobbing and wailing in utter anguish blasted from our TV set through the rest of the house. Immediately I clutched to my heart. Maybe it was the mother in me; maybe it's just that I'm a sensitive soul. Because my sense of hearing was instantly impacted, my heart started racing—in my mind I heard this young girl screaming for her mother.

Consciously choosing not to look at the screen, I shouted to my family to mute it until I was out of earshot. Unfortunately they were completely lost in *Game of Thrones,* unable to hear or care about my request. Frustrated, scared and annoyed, I asked again for the TV to be silenced—but now it was too late. I glimpsed the TV screen—they are massive these days and hard to miss—and the sight of a young girl being murdered completely threw me over the edge.

Racing upstairs, I darted into the shower, hoping to wash away the negative feeling. In the quiet of my room I read up on Energy Fields. In the middle of the night, I woke to the otherworldly sounds of the girl, burning and writhing in pain and agony. The experience of this TV character and the events I'd witnessed—ever so briefly—greatly impacted my psyche. That actress was real to me, and in the darkness of my bedroom I heard her scream out, I saw her scream and I felt her scream as if I was witnessing it in person.

Laying there in the dark, I decided I would let the negative events of the night go, that I was going to take charge of my thoughts.

Sitting up in bed, my mind replayed a "Letting Go" exercise. I envisioned the girl's image and heard her terrifying screams. I pictured myself cupping my hands in front of me, calling to my hands the image, the sound and the feeling I was experiencing. I imagined it in my hands, and no longer in my mind. In my mind's eye, I watched myself lifting my hands high, holding them up to the sky. I imagined the fears, the thoughts, the feelings and the brutal imagery leaving my hands, my space, my presence. I watched them lift higher and higher above my head, through the clouds, into the vast universe, there to be taken away by a powerful angel.

Immediately, I was at peace. I took charge over my thoughts, and with my unbending intent, I fell right back to sleep.

The events of the day can damage us. They can trigger anxiety, fatigue, anger, frustration and many other emotional challenges. The experiences of your day and the people you interact with will affect your emotional health; the effects of negative experiences such as fear, anxiety, sadness, or anger will block the life force energy in your body, your *chi,* your *prana,* your breath. Eventually this negative energy will develop into a disease or a disorder that will be much more difficult to work through.

It is vital to connect with yourself and your thoughts regularly.

Find a process, create a ritual—whether it is meditating, sitting quietly in nature, writing in a journal, or taking a walk. Stay in touch with your thoughts. Take the time to understand your Self. Taking the time to connect will bring clarity. Clarity creates understanding and wisdom, and from wisdom springs peace and joy.

Important Things to Remember:

- Be mindful of your day-to-day thoughts. The negative events of your day can create a negative emotional response. Winning the war in your mind means learning to listen to your personal truths, not a constant soundtrack of negative lies.

- The key to overcoming PTSD is taking back control of your mind, your thoughts and your actions by connecting with your *self* before it feels like the sky is falling.

- Your thoughts become your reality. Negative thoughts create a negative life, a life spinning out of control in a downward spiral. No matter the circumstances, you have the power to take charge of your thoughts. By creating a positive perception about your life and your future, you can be free.

These healing techniques were hard-won lessons for me. After my NDEs, I knew I needed a battle plan, one that would effect and achieve change in every facet of my life. All NDErs need a personal battle plan to start living with purpose, and to shut out the negative noise and traumatic events of the past.

Yet for some, the battle seems unwinnable. For some, the comfort of addiction to substances—especially alcohol and drugs—offers a more effective antidote.

If you need freeing from the monster of addiction, my next chapter was written for you.

11

Healing Addiction After Trauma

THIS IS THE STORY OF MY ADDICTION.

Addiction is a disease—a powerful, serious disease. With addiction comes guilt, disgrace, shame. Shame and addiction often walk arm-in-arm—feeding and fueling each other by feelings of inadequacy, unworthiness, and forming a toxic relationship, an unspeakable bond.

Addiction after an NDE is especially unspeakable.

I don't remember how or when I felt the need to add alcohol and cigarettes to my life. I do remember my first prescription medication—my doctor prescribed Concerta for my ADHD, as I was struggling at work and couldn't focus or concentrate. Later I began taking a combination of Zoloft and Ativan for anxiety and depression. A combination of the two also helped my PTSD.

I was taking all types of prescription medications to *heal* me, to *help* me, but I kept needing to increase the doses. The medication did help the moments I needed them most, but they were not *healing* me, and that is what I needed.

My addiction to smoking had begun earlier.

I *loved* smoking cigarettes. The first brand I'd tried were Virginia Slims Light Menthol. I later changed to Marlboro Lights, which became my cigarette of choice.

In the beginning, I only smoked a couple a day. After the kids were put to bed, I'd sit outside and have two cigarettes—only two, no more. I never smoked when I was pregnant, and on-and-off I'd stop smoking altogether, occasionally for years at a time. I just really *loved* smoking.

I found myself sneaking off to smoke when I started to feel anxious or sad. I'd hide out in our garage, and light up. My trembling hand could never light the cigarette fast enough; I never put one cigarette out before lighting up the next one. I'd sit alone in the quiet, frantically lighting and re-lighting cigarettes, and smoke until the bad feelings passed.

I knew it was a terrible habit—yet puffing on a cigarette was relaxing. When I smoked, my attitude changed, and the perpetual pain I lived with stopped weighing on me.

When I developed anxiety, I started to smoke more and more; when I was in full-blown PTSD, I smoked a lot. Cigarettes relieved my anxiety— or so I thought. The truth is, nicotine fueled my anxiety, and after smoking on and off for years, I realized the cigarettes I was smoking were no longer the innocent smokes of the past—they were much more powerful, and more addictive.

Smoking was an escape for me, my way to avoid life; inhaling and exhaling, I could be alone and be quiet. I didn't think about the anxiety, about my fears: I just smoked and thought about the next time I would be able to smoke.

Yet I knew I was addicted to cigarettes. And I didn't want to die from lung cancer. Quitting smoking would be difficult—on the way to my first healing workshop, I smoked and smoked the whole way there, thinking this would be the last time, that I'd be able to quit. That didn't work, and I remember buying a pack on the way home.

Finally, I was able to quit cold-turkey. I just stopped one day. It was painful—but by this time, I was actively meditating, and felt a desire to fill myself up with Spirit, not carcinogens. After a few days, miraculously my addiction to cigarettes was over. Something else had brought me peace and quiet, something that was much better for me.

I began adding wine to my daily routine when I thought I needed something *more*. More than the cigarettes. More than the pills. Trying to mask my surging anxiety, I would add a glass of wine to my dinner, while watching TV or while I was cooking. Just a couple of glasses at night, to balance my mood, that's all. Alcohol was never as necessary as my cigarettes, or my Ativan, Concerta and Zoloft.

I never considered myself an alcoholic—I never drank to get drunk. I relied on drinking for self-soothing—but I was dependent upon my medications, without which I felt I couldn't survive. The pills were my rescuers, potent enough to mask the emotional pain, powerful enough to blot out the trauma of near-death.

I didn't know any better and I had no idea my body was dependent upon the medications. I never thought I had a problem; I had the best doctors overseeing my care, and my medications were necessary. What was there to worry about? What happened though was my mind and my body began to *believe* that the only way I would be okay, the only way I could be free of my pain and get through the day, was with the medication.

But was I addicted? Did something have control over me, something that needed to be fed and fed?

Indeed.

What I really needed was a release. I needed to share. I needed to let go of what I was holding back. I needed awareness and assurance that the extraordinary feelings from my NDEs were actually gifts—healing gifts.

Recovering from my NDE was as traumatic as the NDE itself. I'd only heard stories about the positive experiences of near-death; no one ever seemed to discuss the negative effects, like anxiety, depression and PTSD. All the stories I'd read or heard were about the amazing accounts of being in the Light, of feeling the unconditional love. I'd experienced those moments too, of course; but I'd suffered trauma to get there.

When I returned from near-death, I needed to talk, to share my fears with somebody. I needed to talk about the blood in Tom's car as it sank into the mud, the fear of my cancer recurring, the despair I felt learning I would lose my breast, and the fear of unseen sepsis infection that invaded my body.

I *wanted,* I *needed,* I *pleaded* and *begged* to share with someone who would understand my experiences, as well as my newly-discovered paranormal gifts. Unable to find understanding or empathy, I remained quiet, never sharing what I longed to release.

Yet even talking about my experience wouldn't have been enough. Nothing was ever enough. Not the wine. Not the pills. Not cigarettes. My soul knew I didn't want to become an alcoholic or an addict, hooked on prescription drugs, or chainsmoking myself into cancer. And I didn't want to end up in rehab. I knew in my soul that I needed to heal, and that it was time.

I was broken. Being broken was my blessing. I was blessed to watch my life crumble into pieces, to fall apart—because in falling apart, I learned to pick myself up.

Trauma had a strong hold on me. Trauma from an NDE can be a major contributing factor in addiction.

When an NDEr experiences trauma in their brush with death, that negative experience can have a lifelong impact. Further, when that trauma is repeated—such as flashbacks of my car accident, or repeated nightmares about my battle with sepsis—it makes a person more susceptible to seeking escape from that recurring trauma, through substance abuse, mood-altering drugs, or other harmful behavior.

When trauma and the negative emotions that come along with it go unresolved, deeper and more serious issues can take root.

Trauma symptoms differ. Trauma sufferers can experience sleep disorders, nightmares, flashbacks, anxiety and depression, and episodes where they feel disconnected from reality. Excessive trauma can leave an NDEr predisposed or prey to addiction.

For decades, researchers have been studying the connection between trauma and addiction, in order to understand why so many NDErs have histories of drug or alcohol abuse.

The theories behind the common connection of addiction and trauma are complicated. People struggling to manage anxiety and trauma in their lives turn to substances or risky behavior to self-medicate. Sedating by alcohol or stimulating by drugs soon becomes just another problem in the trauma survivor's life. Before long, their "cure" stops working or has them locked in its addictive grasp. The suffering NDE survivor is trapped in an even deeper, more sinister battle.

Addiction to prescription or street drugs brings another level of danger. Driving a car while impaired, the risk of physical violence and sexual abuse, criminal acquaintances, hazardous neighborhoods—the addicted brain will go to any lengths, to get what it needs and craves.

There may be a genetic component connecting those who've survived an NDE and those with addictive tendencies, though no definitive conclusion has been attained by research.

Sometimes, years of self-medicating dulls the memory of an NDEr's trauma, bringing a partial solution along with addiction. Unfortunately, continuing to avoid resolution of their near-death trauma almost guarantees ongoing torture and suffering.

Dealing with a traumatic experience is demanding work. Trapped in the fog of drugs and alcohol, it is nearly impossible. Working with a therapist in individual or group counseling to address the underlying unresolved trauma may help. Assessment by a skilled therapist, to determine how the addiction craving can be overcome, can help the NDEr devise a treatment plan or approach. Working on getting back to a sober or healthy lifestyle, at the same time as resolving NDE trauma while adding positive coping skills, gives the NDEr the tools for a more hopeful, more productive life.

Terrified of the past, and terrified of the future. Living in fear of experiencing another event, and living in fear none will ever come. Fear and dread that one has no control. This is the life of an NDEr who's experienced trauma.

The NDEr's day-after-day struggle to keep traumatic memories of the event locked away can be exhausting. After months and years, defense mechanisms weaken, even the best coping skills can become overwhelmed, and more radical forms of comfort become necessary.

The highway between substance addiction and trauma can become wide open, under these conditions. The trauma of their NDE increases the risk of abuse or addiction, increasing the likelihood that the experiencer becomes involved in more and more high-risk behavior, abusing drugs or alcohol, gambling or unhealthy sexual behavior or overeating in a desperate effort to cope with their traumatic event, in an attempt to soothe their emotional distress and find comfort.

It makes perfect sense that an experiencer flooded with shame, unworthiness and anxiety after an NDE needs a source of comfort. The traumatized NDEr senses an insatiable craving for relief or fulfillment; their sense of emptiness after a near-death episode is overwhelming. Finding instant relief from substances or risky behavior only leaves them feeling more unworthy, more vulnerable.

Clearly, NDE stress and trauma can be linked to addiction. Trauma impacts an experiencer's ability to cope with anxiety and stress. When anxiety and stress become unbearable, overwhelming and terrifying, it often leads to desperate measures. Too often, those desperate measures lead to addiction.

There is an upside, however.

Given the undeniable connection between addiction and NDE trauma, NDErs need more compassionate programs for healing. Addiction and NDE trauma need to be treated as interconnected. Without an avenue to help NDErs cope with their terror, shame, unworthiness and isolation, there's no upside to becoming sober. Yet solace and healing from their experience without addiction is possible, so long as a healthy recovery outweighs the benefits and refuge of their addiction.

HEALING ADDICTION AFTER TRAUMA

When addiction gets its grip on a trauma victim, the implementation of a positive personal action plan becomes critical. Healing from addiction after an NDE requires an even more intense and strategically-minded action plan.

1. Awareness

Stress led me to my addiction. Stress later sent me on a voyage of positive self-discovery. I was forced to discover what life-stress was causing me to negatively self-soothe. Little did I know I was struggling with pent-up dark emotions; I thought it was the stress of my job as a founder and executive director of a non-profit supporting cancer patients. *Maybe the day-to-day interactions with patients who were sick was the reason I was so stressed out, and needed to smoke, take pills and drink wine,* I reasoned. Or maybe it was managing my son's significant learning challenges that made it impossible for him to be in a regular classroom. Or maybe my husband switching jobs…or my father being sick.

In the end, it was none of those things that brought me on my knees to my cigarettes or my bottle of wine. When I became aware that it was my emotional wounds that needed soothing, that they were blocking my Light, I was able to heal.

Become aware of what is blocking your Light. Ask yourself: *What is unresolved within me?* The stress in our daily lives is usually obvious; *why* we can't handle this stress is usually not. What are you filling yourself with that is taking your energy, disallowing the peace, the clarity and the power of the Light to come in? Becoming aware will help you find the answers you need.

2. Develop Healthy Habits that Promote Healing

Trauma leads NDErs to being more vulnerable; suffering significant trauma, or the constant replaying of that trauma through PTSD, they are become susceptible to addiction. Developing healthy habits soon after their trauma may help avoid addiction.

Healthy habits after trauma could be as simple as incorporating healthier food, rich in healing vitamins that can increase your energy. Exercising, moving the energy in your body, promotes healing on many levels.

I created a daily schedule and incorporated healthy self-care habits throughout the day. It was a process. I needed to learn what was *healthy* and what habits would be beneficial for me. At times, my shadow side would surface and tell me I was being selfish or lazy. It wasn't long before I was able to silence my shadow side, and listen to the voice of my soul.

This took time. I'd made time throughout the day for my cigarettes; I'd made time for my glass of wine after dinner. Over time, I replaced my bad healing habits with healthy new ones. I replaced my wine with a hot cup of tea and chose to schedule walks outside and meditation, instead of a cigarette break.

I allowed myself to be the priority, giving myself permission to take the time for myself. I suggest you schedule your exercise, meditation or health food shopping around the same time every day. Create a routine, a regimen. Your mind and your body will appreciate the reassuring, reenergizing ritual.

3. Get Enough!

Make a priority to get enough of the simple things— fresh air, food, water and rest. Listen to your body. What is it asking of you? Food, sleep or quiet? Try eating consciously by asking your body what it needs for fuel. Healing from a trauma is not the time to start a new fad diet. Get plenty of nourishment. Some people mistake a low blood sugar attack for an anxiety or panic attack, as they can feel eerily similar. Eat at regular hours and 4 to 6 small meals a day. If your inner self is stressed from trauma, soothing it with healthy habits will promote healing on many levels—but only if you *get enough!*

4. Love Yourself

Sounds easy, doesn't it?

I never loved myself. I never liked my body; I wished I looked different. *Is my hair okay? Is my voice too loud?* I never enjoyed time alone, with myself. Insecure about everything relating to *me* made me a miserable, unstable wreck.

*Loving yourself…*It took me a while to grasp this concept. Maybe because I understood *loving yourself* to mean being conceited, selfish and self-absorbed. No way I wanted to be any of those! But later in life, I discovered there were two parts to me. In order to love my *Self,* I had to understand my parts—the outside self and my inside Self. I came to an understanding and gained knowledge about myself, enabling me to accept myself and to love the parts of me.

Overcoming addiction starts with *loving yourself.*

My Outside Self is worth love. For instance, I love it that my legs can take me for long walks or for a run. I love my legs for allowing me to move and be free and go where I want or need to go. And my arms—I love my arms for allowing me to eat and hold my children and my husband.

How can we *not* love our bodies for what they provide us! We must appreciate our body for all that it does, not for what it is.

Once I understood what my true and highest Self's intention and purpose was, I grew to love myself, both the inside and the outside.

I believe loving ourselves is one of the hardest concepts for many of us to grasp. Especially if you never felt love, or received a loving touch as a child, or heard the words, "I love you."

There is the idea that we can only love ourselves as much as others love us. The truth is, we can receive as much love as we feel. We must love ourselves to the degree we want to feel and receive love. If we are searching and hoping for love, it will be difficult to find until we have found it within ourselves.

Loving ourselves in addiction is critical. Loving ourselves allows us to experience a greater depth of love. Love becomes more intense, more passionate, more powerful. Many of us exist just giving love, loving everyone and every creature. We open our hearts to others, because we want to, and it makes us feel good. But that's not the way our bodies work: The energy that beats our heart is the same energy that gives and receives love. What our bodies wish to receive is that which we give out. We need to remember to give and receive in all areas equally—to love and to be loved.

There's no doubt that most people are going to hit a roadblock on the journey to loving themselves. It's a process; it's hard work. To experience joy, to find clarity and to know your life's intention, you must begin with yourself. If you are struggling with the concept of loving, you will struggle with releasing the power your addiction holds over you.

So often we look for the fulfillment outside ourselves: Food, new cars, sex, drugs, shopping, alcohol. The truth is we can find so much fulfillment and love and attention and joy by connecting with our Self.

Never forget: If you're trapped in addiction, you're in warfare. You're in a private, personal war zone. Once you begin fighting to take that turf away from your addiction, your addiction will fight to keep it. But loving yourself is your greatest weapon. Loving yourself is an offensive action. Loving yourself is how you can battle the chokehold of addiction—how you can face your fears, your trials, your troubles, your traumas and win the battle.

Important Things to Remember:

- Start loving yourself by just being gentle with yourself and learning to forgive yourself.

- If you need to hear the words "I love you" from someone, then express those words out loud to another, asking them to say those words to you. Tell them you love them back; create the loving language that they need to learn.

- Your physical self is the container, the shield, the protector of your true inner self. Shield your inner self by rejecting the chatter of discouragement; persist instead in the habit of sharing encouraging messages with yourself.

- *Give* love. Giving love is as important as receiving love.

- Create a relationship with yourself. Take yourself to the park for a picnic; see a good TV show or have a fine dinner. It might seem lonely, because you are alone. But in solitude we learn to truly know ourselves; in solitude with yourself, you can be joyful.

There is no greater agony than bearing
an untold story inside you.
—Maya Angelou

Overcoming addiction isn't easy. Nobody loves an addict. Nobody wants an addict around. Desperation to release ourselves from untold trauma leads some NDErs to the most dangerous sources of relief—risky behavior and substance abuse. Abuse slowly becomes addiction, then becomes an ever-tightening spiral.

In overcoming addiction, look for comfort and strength within yourself—and look for self-love within the Light. That's the untold story that is waiting to be shared—the story of how you beat addiction, rediscovered and reengaged your true gifts, and used your redemption story to heal others.

Whatever trauma you're dealing with can be beaten. My story is proof of this—though I confess there were times when the hidden gifts of the Light exhausted my endurance, and the journey to harness them left me drained and empty.

In Part Three of my story, I'll share how I discovered my hidden NDE gifts, and how you can pursue and harness your own.

PART THREE

INTO THE LIGHT

12

The Gift of Healing After an NDE

I SPENT YEARS SEARCHING.

Searching for peace, for health, for happiness. Searching to heal my anxiety, my fearfulness, my depression and PTSD. I was searching for my life's purpose and for an answer to the always-burning question in my heart: *Why had I survived these near-deaths? Why had I encountered the Light? And why had I been released back to life?*

Never finding the answers I sought only deepened my anxiety and depression. *Am I crazy?* I wondered. I felt confused, the world around me collapsing, never able to find the simple truth I was searching for.

It wasn't until years later that I realized the truth—that I'd received some special life-changing gifts from my NDEs.

Awareness of these gifts was slow to come, and impossible at first to perceive.

After my first brush with the Light, I received the gift of clairsentience, often referred to as a "the sixth sense"—the ability to feel the present, past or future physical and emotional states of others, in your own body, and while still using the normal five senses (smell, vision, touch, hearing and taste). My body had become a resonating tool, an intuitive instrument playing the feelings of others.

After my second encounter with the Light, this gift would be enhanced to an even higher degree, and the urge and push of Spirit to use it would become more pronounced.

I believe Spirit had guided my journey. My guides knew I needed to heal myself before I could effect change in the world. As I began studying Deborah King's LifeForce Energy Healing®, to treat my physical, emotional, mental and spiritual wounds, I was in training. I was becoming a teacher and a healer, a Lightworker eager to serve.

The healing process—letting go of all the negative past I was holding onto, and the future that was not serving me, then seeking forgiveness by examining my core beliefs through daily freewriting and journaling—was *hard work*! It was hard to feel, to let go and release! Daily I reminded myself: *It will take time, and dedication. It will take an unbending intent, to heal.* I had to purge the dark within me so my healing Light would shine.

The words I wrote in journaling became my refuge among the noise of the world. Spending time in nature and in my meditations supplied the awareness I needed. After I shed the toxic emotions of shame and guilt, I began carving out room for clarity—in clarity, I knew I would find the answers to my questions. Through the voices and messages in nature and through the voice of my soul in meditation, I received all I needed. No longer would I need to *search* for the answers—I never needed to *search* for the Light, because the answers and the connection to Source was waiting *within* me all along!

Right in the center of my being, my heart held the peace I longed for. My heart held the answers to all my burning questions. It would be in my own purged and purified heart that I found the Light I longed to return to—it was in my own heart that I found all I'd ever need to heal. In my heart, I found that love restores balance. In my heart, I found that compassion heals. I understood through the voice of my heart and my soul that my journey was far from over, that in order to heal, I needed to discover the love within myself, to love myself unconditionally. In order to honor the Light, I needed to walk the Light's path.

Staying on the path might not be easy, I thought to myself hesitantly. But against all odds,. I did it.

THE GIFT OF HEALING OTHERS AFTER AN NDE

I now work as a Healer and a Teacher. Using the LifeForce Energy Healing® technique, using my Light, I connect with the Light and energy of the Divine. Connecting to the Light, I allow its energy to move through me, pulse through my own body, conducting the healing energy that will be released through my heart, through my hands.

After receiving the initial gifts of intuition and clairsentience through my NDE, I began developing two other healing gifts—clairaudience and clairvoyance. My Light—which once felt like a small speck, a tiny spark of fledgling light yearning to shine in the darkness—became a beacon. When our Lights meet, our connection can effect good.

This is my calling, my purpose: To continue evolving consciously; to expand my fledgling energy field; to brighten my Light so I am able to attract the highest and greatest healing; and to allow this power to radiate and conduct through me and create the healing change in others.

Each day offers new gifts, new joys, new challenges. Even as a healer, I am changing and evolving all the time.

You are changing and evolving all the time, too.

Had it not been for my NDE, I would not have received these special gifts of the Light. Using the gifts of healing offered by your NDE, you can tap into the regenerative healing energy of the Light, too. Your Light can grow, expand and evolve to a powerful, life-giving force that connects with the Light and energy of the Divine. Your Light can connect with the force that frees you, the force that heals you, healing yourself and then others with a heart full of unconditional love and compassion.

DEVELOPING THE GIFTS OF HEALING

Dream with me for a moment. Relax and imagine a reality in which you've been given the resources to heal others—their troubled minds, their broken souls, their dysfunctional hearts.

The principles I learned from the Light—the principles I will share in this chapter—have the potential to turn those dreams, and the gifts we all have the power to develop, into reality.

1. Become Heart-Centered.

Make it a daily practice to go to your heart. Try this exercise:

Find a spot to make yourself comfortable. Close your eyes and take a few deep clearing breaths, breathing in through your nose and out through your mouth. After a few breaths, place your attention on your heart. Place your hand over it. With your eyes closed, feel your heartbeat. Feel the rhythm of your heart and listen to the sound of your internal music. How do you sound? Using your imagination, go into your body. In front of your heart are double doors. Taking your fingers, tap lightly on your breastbone and knock gently on the doors. As the doors open, you are greeted and welcomed. Ask yourself: Who is answering the door? Who is there, in your heart? Is the Divine there? Are there angels? Guides? Spirit animals? If you wish someone to be there, call for them to come. Who do you wish to center in your heart? Who do you want to guide you? Ask them: *Come. Come into my heart.*

The heart is the center of healing. When I was wounded, and my healer took me inside my heart, it was cold, dark and empty. I believed that everything I needed to heal was in the outside world, when the truth was the opposite: It was all within me. I discovered the power of my heart, the power the heart has to heal. After years of searching the outside world for the peace and light I craved, I found it all waiting within me, in my center.

My heart.

Living a heart-centered life has enhanced my gift of healing. I make it a practice to check in to my heart and feel the energy, the restorative power and presence of the Divine.

Become heart-centered. Live your life heart-centered.

2. Surrender to Spirit

When I discovered the gift of healing and other paranormal gifts, I made a vow to surrender to Spirit. I allowed myself to experience and accept the messages and signs I was receiving. I stopped passing judgment on myself; I stopped questioning and labeling whether something I was experiencing was *real* or not. And I connected with my guides.

Connecting with my guides enhanced my gifts. I was able communicate with them—but only so long as I was patient, and never rushed. I never placed a condition or a request on my guides, never asking them to *show me you are with me*. I understood that I needed to be present, and wait. I needed to surrender to the process—a process I would never control or own. I needed to allow myself to listen deeper, to feel deeper, and to believe the experience was true.

Learning to surrender to Spirit, I discovered the enormous support and guidance I could receive. I waited patiently for my guides to make themselves known, and then I listened quietly with my body and heart, waiting until they taught me the universal tongue we would speak, the language of our communication.

Begin now to develop open communication with your guides. Build the language. Trust in the process. Manifest the conversations and you will find your gift of healing and other NDE gifts unfolding exponentially.

3. Love Unconditionally

The one issue I never had in my life was with *loving*. I loved others deeply—it was only myself I couldn't love. I cared for everyone and everything, except me. For most of my life I poured my heart energy into the world, but never allowed myself to receive. I loved others and everything else in the world unconditionally—all except me.

It was only after my second NDE that the Light taught me to love myself, openly and fearlessly. I became an expression of the Light's unconditional love, pouring out my natural ability to love on others, and on myself.

If you want to enhance or develop your gift of healing, enhance your ability to love. Open your heart, love others, love animals and all living things. Love your friends and your enemies equally, and love yourself unconditionally. When you stop loving conditionally, you stop judging; when you stop judging, you begin to see everything and everyone — including yourself—just as we all are, perfect.

To experience and to share unconditional love, NDErs and others must perceive themselves as equally and fully loving of each and all, be openly generous, and excited about the potential and wonder of each person they see.

MANIFESTING GIFTS AFTER AN NDE

It took years before I finally understood the many loving gifts I'd received from my NDE—the gifts of intuition, of healing, of deepened compassion. A gift of the near-death experience itself, the act of nearly dying, was my connection to the Light. That pinpoint of bright light that evolves into a massive energy filled with infinite love is the same place I'm transported to now during my daily meditation. I connect with the same energy and fill myself with its unconditional love and compassion, letting go of any negative emotional baggage, anxiety, sadness.

I have since discovered that this connection to the Light is there for all of us, NDErs and non-NDErs alike. The gift of the Light is meant for everyone.

For years, I never knew that others had experienced similar near-death episodes. I never realized I'd experienced near-death in Tom's car; I failed to realize it until after my second NDE. It wasn't until I discovered energy healing and meditation that I found the connection I'd encountered in near-death was available to me, in life.

I remember reading a few excerpts from the book *Embraced by the Light* by Betty Eadie. In her book, Eadie described what she witnessed during her NDE—people working in peace and serenity, and the beautiful room they occupied. Dropping the book from my trembling hands, I nearly cried tears of joy—*My God, it is all true!* I thought. Eadie described a place where all could connect, where all could come to find the purpose of their life, and to hear Divine messages—not just the dead, but the living too!

This experience reflected my own. When I nearly died of sepsis, I experienced feeling outside of my body. I looked above myself in the hospital bed, seeing people arrive to visit me—then suddenly I was hurled back inside my body. My insides, my blood flow, my heart, all felt slowed down, sedated, yet there was a renewed sense of energy on the outside.

In that moment, the Light was right before me, like a door I needed to enter. *I don't need to say goodbye to my family,* I realized, melting into this thought. I thought of all the women I'd met during my cancer treatment—those with terminal cancer and those with young children. I was comforted, knowing *this* is what those women felt: Peace. Letting that peace take root, I relaxed, knowing when I crossed-over that my own children would be protected.

In my death, I felt connected, alive and well. Going to the Light felt like a necessary journey, someplace I needed to be. Joyfully I went.

After my return from near-death, I spent a good amount of time anxious and depressed. I'd found the gift of the Light, and I wanted it back. It was difficult to transition from the Light's unconditional love to the hardships of real life. My religious beliefs changed dramatically. Being raised Catholic, with an understanding that when I died, my life would be over and my soul would live in Heaven, became expanded. I didn't have to be perfect, I didn't always need to be a good girl, or always do the right thing, to get to the Light. I could make mistakes, I could make bad decisions, I could try and fail, and still be connected to the Light. We live, we suffer, we survive, and we die to get to the Light.

In my suffering, I learned how to heal; in nearly dying, I learned how to thrive and how to access the gifts I received in life.

Although the NDE caused me anxiety, depression, PTSD and addiction, that wasn't the experience's purpose. Once I was able to discern what that purpose was, I was able to manifest the gifts of the Light—gifts that are available to each and every one of us, every day.

How can you connect with these gifts? Here's how:

1. Release Negative and Toxic Energy

To connect with the Light, it's important to connect with those who already live in the Light—those who are kind, compassionate and loving. Connect with non-judgmental people, with those who believe you are worthy to receive the Light, and the power of grace, love and forgiveness the Light brings.

Light attracts light, and Dark attracts dark.

If you are filled with negativity, or toxic emotions such as fear, guilt, shame, or worry, you are blocking the Light. You are filling your body with darkness, leaving little room for the regenerative power of the Light.

There's one way to connect with the Light: Make room for it. Take the time, and the patience, getting to know what is blocking you from the Light. Are you angry or afraid? Do you harbor shame? Do you hold onto guilt? Release those toxic emotions to the Light.

When you feel safe, and no longer fear life, when you allow yourself to experience joy, when you own your power and love yourself and speak your truth and believe that all is possible, you will be surrounded in the Light!

Let go of the dark, and choose the Light.

2. Your Imagination is Your Reality

For years, I was told I had a wild imagination. I'd see people who had passed a way, hear messages from them in the beyond and think I was imagining it. If I mentioned the experience to someone, they stared at me as if I had ten heads! Because of this, I rarely ever mentioned my paranormal abilities.

I was wrong. Imagination is sacred. Imagination is your reality.

After my second NDE I was at a cooking demonstration. During this time, I had the strange perception that I'd changed; my abilities to see and sense things felt beyond the ordinary. As this woman was teaching us to cook homemade pasta, I felt a *tap-tap-tap* on my shoulder. Turning around, I experienced a vision of an old Italian woman, telling me, "That's my stuff! That's *my* stuff!" Clearly I understood: It was her recipe, her method of cooking, yet she was not on the cover of the cookbook! Instead, there was a photograph of her daughter and her granddaughter, the one who was now cooking for us.

Oh Lord, I thought, *how do I help this poor woman?* She nagged and nagged me, and refused to leave me alone. I couldn't take it anymore, so I blurted out to the woman cooking, "That's your great grandmother's stuff! And she is *not* happy that she's not on the cover of the book!" Everyone went silent. The cook stopped. All eyes were on me until the woman's granddaughter spoke up. "You're right," she admitted, "They were hers. How did you know that?" Embarrassed, I shrugged. "Just a guess."

Later that night in private she came to me, holding a photo in an album—it was the old woman tapping me on the shoulder, her great grandmother.

Was it my imagination? Or my reality?

I look back and think of the years I lost, worrying about what people would think or what they would say. The truth is my imagination *was* my reality. What I saw in visions, what I witnessed in the shadows, what I heard in the whispers—it was all true. I'd never allowed myself the opportunity to believe it was all possible.

Opening myself to believing my imagination was my reality opened a deeper connection with myself, and with the Light.

3. Live Compassionately Toward All

We are all one. We are all connected. We are consciously connected. Our thoughts have energy, our words have energy and our eyes have energy.

Being compassionate is a step toward being one with the Light. Compassion begins in our hearts, and manifests itself in our actions.

When you think about someone, be they friend or enemy, think about them with compassion. When you speak about someone, use the voice of compassion, not criticism or judgment. When you see someone on the street, see with the eyes of compassion. When you see a homeless person, don't rush to judgment. See them as part of the Light.

Begin *now*. Begin a practice of *being* compassionate. Live as though you are the other person—feel them, empathize with them, as if they were you. Have compassion for all living things. There is only unconditional love and compassion in the Light.

If you want to connect with the Light, you must live *according to the Light*.

4. Open Your Heart

Opening our heart does not come naturally or easily, for most of us. Most of us like to have control over our heart. Yet if we want the Light to pour into our lives, we must entrust the Light with an open heart.

The good news is we don't need to fear opening our heart and giving control of it to the Light. There is nothing more freeing than opening our heart, and accepting the Light as its eternal guide, its benevolent master.

The voice of the heart is kind and gentle. The voice of the heart is pure love. Your heart is your personal connection to Source, to Spirit, to all that is.

We don't get to the Light from our head—we get to the Light from our hearts. Open your heart and connect to the Light and the healing gifts it provides.

The only hope we have of manifesting our gifts is by loosening our death grip on control, and by acknowledging that everything we have and everything we are is a gift from the Light.

ENHANCING YOUR INTUITION AND YOUR PSYCHIC GIFTS

AFTER AN NDE

Few NDE topics ignite the kind of heated, passionate discussion as the topic of psychic gifts. First, let's talk about one of mine: Intuition.

It's true that my enhanced intuition came from my NDE—yet you don't need to experience near-death to receive the gift of intuition, or the many other extraordinary paranormal gifts life offers us. The first step is *awareness*. We get caught up in the illusion that paranormal gifts are supernatural—not true. Rather, we all can tap into this universal energy, and use it.

The paranormal gifts we receive—regardless of how they come to us—are meant to be used. Spirit is asking us, nudging us, begging us to assist in making or creating good in this world.

When I received the gift of enhanced intuition, initially I rejected it. *What makes you so special?* I asked myself. *How do you know what people are thinking?* My ego would get in the way of Spirit's work; because of this, I was unreliable to Spirit.

Luckily, Spirit kept nudging me, and never gave up on me.

As I said, our gifts are meant to be used—to effect change and create good in the world. I'm certain the reason behind my second near-death experience was to hammer and bombard me with this message: *Cathy, use the incredible gifts you've received!* Suddenly I felt the urge, the need, the burning desire to use them, although I didn't know how.

I had no clue, no idea how to even begin to use my gifts. Confused, I turned to my energy healing lessons, yearning to release whatever was blocking my progress. Releasing these blocks gave the gifts an opportunity to rise to the surface. Using the information I learned about myself, at last I could discern my NDE's gifts, their purpose and how to use them. Finally I was able to stop fearing and dismissing them, and put my gifts into action.

I began to *discern* the difference between my enhanced intuition and my own fleeting thoughts. I began to *accept* the instant information as a blessing, not a plague or a curse. I began to *accept* the information as my guide, and as I was intuitively guided I would act accordingly.

As I did, my enhanced intuition began to manifest even more; as it did, my enhanced compassion, clairsentience and clairvoyance also intensified. I became energized by my psychic gifts, lifted up by these instruments of the Light.

Many other paranormal gifts can be perceived after a near-death experience—automatic writing, telepathy, channeling, levitation, precognition, psychoscopy, retrocognition, remote viewing, telekinesis. And more.

Each NDEr has their own personal story and unique paranormal gifts. Whether or not you have had a near-death experience, each of us has the ability to tap into extraordinary, paranormal gifts. Rather than fight against them, why not increase, enhance and intensity those abilities? You can become a powerful conduit by following these simple steps:

1. Stay Grounded and Present

To attract the resources and support your paranormal gift, you must be grounded. You must be rooted. You must be present in your mind and in your body. Take the time to ground yourself each day—take a walk out in nature, sit under a tree, walk barefoot, or intentionally root your feet into the ground. Make sure you are in an environment that enhances your connection to quiet, to inner serenity, to peace, to Spirit.

2. Immerse Yourself in Meditation

Prayer is speaking to or asking to receive something; meditation is listening to or listening for the answers, the meaning, the understanding you need in life. In meditation, your mind discovers clarity; the information you have been searching for becomes clear. It is in meditation that you will receive the awareness you need to nurture your gifts. Create a daily meditation ritual, quiet your mind, immerse yourself. And listen.

3. Foster a Deep Devotion

It is my devotion to Source and my devotion to healing that enhances my healing gifts. I am devoted to the process of being present here in this lifetime, and effecting change for the good of others and all living creatures. My pure love of others and my joy of restoring them fuels my devotion and increases my healing abilities.

4. Commit to Your Guides

Take the time to connect and commit to the Presence who wants to work through you. Ask your guide: *What is my purpose here on Earth? How do you intend for me to use my gifts?*

My pure love of others, my joy of helping and my commitment to my guides has intensified my healing abilities and the gifts I received after my NDE. When I first encountered my guides, I rejected my gifts, out of fear. With time, consistency, and trust, a bond formed, a language developed, and the purpose of my extraordinary gifts were not only revealed, they were enhanced, and incorporated into my daily life.

Ultimately, my gifts from the Light offered me the opportunity to embrace true freedom—a life free from stress and anxiety, and a life which honored the Light.

The power of our gifts can't manifest itself, unless we first give ourselves to the Light. As we grow closer to the Light, we become the steward, the manager and the servant of our gift.

Though I've sometimes stumbled with my gift, there has always been one constant rescuer I've turned to, when I'm drowning with internal dialogue I can't control. It has been the soundtrack to my life for as long as I can remember. When the world whispers of my insecurity, when it screams my loudest self-defeating thoughts, I turn to it.

That is the healing, restorative power of prayer.

THE HEALING POWER OF PRAYER

Just say the words and Your Soul Shall be Healed.
—Matthew 8:8

I remember my first-grade religion book; the back page was filled with each of the prayers students were told to memorize. One by one, I would study and memorize them. I knew the verses, word for word, and I prayed them.

Later, when I was tested in life, these words returned to me. When life became more than I could manage, I prayed. I prayed hard, because prayer was all I had.

When I was drowning in sorrow, these words of prayer felt like a breath of life-giving air as I rose out of deep water. Alone in the darkness, my prayers would be the shimmering light. Prayer filled me with a surge of comfort and peace—an energy that would fill my soul, providing just enough hope to carry on another day.

Prayer was my lifejacket, my lifeline, my light before there was a Light.

Prayer was my escape, the tunnel that swept me out of the shadowy darkness and into the Light, into peace.

Prayer brought me closer to the Light, became the air that allowed me to soar. I encourage you, when wracked by the anguish of anxiety, by the constant stress of depression, by the crippling fear of PTSD and the pain of releasing your addiction, to use these words and to be healed by them:

Pray in thanksgiving when you are happy.

Pray in despair for hope.
Pray in tough times for grace, and in dark times for light.
Pray in the morning for guidance and at night in gratitude.
Pray for safety and for joy.
Pray for light and for love.
Pray for the right words.
Pray for insight to see beyond pain.
Pray for all these things.
Pray for yourself.
And pray in thanksgiving, for all that is.
Just pray. Be heard. Be healed. Be at peace.
Pray.

EPILOGUE

A Light Ahead on the Road

There once was a time when talking about my NDEs left me shaken, crippled with insecurity, battered by fear. Thankfully, those days are over. Now I enjoy sharing the story of my NDEs. When people ask if my NDEs changed me, I respond with a confident, joyful *Yes!*

My story is not just about my near-death experiences. It is not just a chronicle of the life I once had—a life filled with pain, self-condemnation, depression, anxiety. It is about *surviving* that pain, that agony, and overcoming. My story is about living with dark emotions such as shame and guilt, and how they created illness in my body—yet in the end, the Light of my NDE transformed and healed me. I shared these parts of me in *Dying to Live* to inspire people like you, to uplift you, to free you, to heal you and to energize, motivate and empower you to move through life with grace and perseverance.

And *faith*.

My life has evolved from the choices I made to respond positively to life, instead of just reacting to death.

It took time, but over time I was able to manifest the healing gifts I received after my NDEs. In order to become my purpose, I needed to restore myself and let go of the pain I suffered in my past. I chose healthy new behaviors that would open my body and mind to healing energies. I chose to love myself unconditionally, which opened my heart to love all living creatures unconditionally. I chose to look at myself and others through the eyes of empathy and compassion.

I have chosen to embrace my near-death experiences—to love and embrace my NDE, and to nurture the gifts of healing, clairsentience, clairvoyance and enhanced intuition that I received from the Light.

I have chosen to let the Light do its work through the sharing of my story. The 18-year-old girl who came back from death has become the Light's fully-awakened messenger.

I have chosen not to die, but in experiencing death to really *live*.

During all my years of trauma, I thought I was alone. I never was. Much as I thought I had disconnected from life, from my friends and family, I never did. I was surrounded by my guides and the angels who walked with me every day. I never felt the power to live my own truths, until I found that I *had* to live my own truths. I never had the courage or the power or the self-esteem to admit that I'd talked with Spirit, or with those who have passed on, or that the Light I encountered through my NDE is working through me to heal and bring change. But I do now.

You are not alone.

Hear those words, if you hear nothing else in this book.

Deborah King's LifeForce Energy Healing® changed my life. It saved me. It was in my healing, the journey from pain and suffering to peace, that I discovered who I was all along.

You can be saved and healed, too. All it takes is reconnecting with your purpose, taking your own journey of self-discovery, and finding your voice.

I lost my voice as a child. This lost voice continued into adulthood. Now I am a speaker—a messenger of Energy Healing. Speaking my truths and sharing my knowledge and my experience heals others. I also opened a small energy healing practice in my hometown.

When I was searching for my office space, the man leading me through the building from floor to floor became curious about my practice. "What are you? A witch?" he finally asked.

His question stopped me dead in my tracks. I chuckled to myself, thinking, *I probably was, in another lifetime.*

"No," I said, feeling his urgency for an answer. "I'm just Cathy, a healer, helping others discover their own path."

I'm not sure when I first saw my Source, my God again; it was a process. The more I healed, the higher I rose toward my calling, and the more I heard and understood my unique purpose.

Through my LFEH courses, I changed, I recovered strength and purpose, and mended old wounds on every level. Every now and then I feel the old anxiety creep in. I ground myself, I take a walk and I remember my mother Ash tree telling me: *You have enough.* Feeling at one with nature I remember: *I have to make sure I have all I need, before I can help, before I can heal anyone else.*

The greatest gift I gave myself was the opportunity to *be me.* To allow myself whatever it was I needed, to heal.

Ask yourself: What is it that *I* need, to heal? Are you physically wounded, mentally wounded, spiritually wounded, emotionally wounded? Ask yourself: What are my wounds? And how can they be healed?

What I learned in studying energy healing is this: We have it all *already*. We have everything we need to heal—the key to healing is *becoming aware* of what *it* is. What is blocking us? What are we are holding onto, that we need to let go of? *Ask,* and you shall receive. We need to allow ourselves permission to receive the nutrients we need—the energy from the sun, the rejuvenating light of the moon, the quiet serenity in meditation— and then be okay with *not doing it all*; be okay with saying, *Help me,* or *I cannot do it, I can't help you, there is not enough of me today.*

Remember you have all of that power already. You are full of it—the bold questions, the brave answers, the awareness. It's all in your heart. Go into yourself, and ask yourself, *What is it that's holding me back?*

The knowing, the awareness is healing itself. Then allow yourself *to be.* Allow yourself to grieve, to mourn, to cry, to laugh, to sing.

To live.

As I was walking down the brick sidewalk to my office, I looked up and saw a woman, a new client, waiting for me. As we locked eyes, my energy connected with her. She greeted me, well-outfitted and stylish. She had strikingly-beautiful, luxurious grey hair, the color of an overcast sky. Immediately my impression of her shifted, and she appeared to me as a Native American medicine woman. I knew she was a healer of some kind, at some point in many of her lifetimes.

We entered the office. We sat. We spoke. Her story was shocking, and behind her courage and truth, was anguish, anger, pain. I felt tears begin to surface, sensing the years of unacknowledged sorrow locked in her body.

My second chakra ached and throbbed with stabbing pain. I knew what she was about to reveal. She had been sexually molested throughout her childhood by her father. She had told almost no one. Instead, she had kept her secret pain hidden.

As this woman spoke, I felt the presence of centuries of Native Americans surround her. I saw puma cats circle and protect her. I knew she was divinely guided; during all her trials, during all her suffering, she was strong, and she was never alone.

Many times, she said, her power was taken. Gang-raped as a teen, she became pregnant before the age of 20. So much suffering she endured, she cried out, so much she'd been robbed of, all for the sake of healing! *She will be a healer again,* I told myself. In this lifetime, she will change lives with the compassion she developed from the years of suffering, from the pain she endured.

She sat beside me, stoic, stone-faced, speaking in a matter-of -fact tone while releasing year after year of intense heartache, years of emotions stored deep into her first and second chakras. Quietly I listened. The lower healing was happening as we sat. Using unbending intent, the connection with the many guides in the room, the Light of Christ, and the techniques of LFEH, her pain was released from its prison. Centuries of Native Americans moved ceremoniously around her, dancing, smudging, wailing and speaking sounds of healing. They wanted her restored; they wanted her to restore others. And so it happened. The tears erupted, and ran down her cheeks, but they were clear, pure and perfect.

I mentioned to her that I felt she was in PTSD as a result of a recent hospital stay, receiving treatment for a lung condition. This sparked old hidden emotions, the decades-old memory of her long hospital stay as a child. She had suffered a hip condition, most likely the result of the significant sexual trauma at the hands of her own father. Her roommate was a sick boy, and during the dark night, they would talk and share stories to ease their fear—but their conversations were always interrupted by a cruel night nurse who would storm in and wheel her crib into a linen closet to silence their talking.

As she described the dark closet and linens and the way they smelled, the way they were stacked, I felt in my own body the knowing, the sensing, the anxiety of never feeling safe, never knowing protection. In my mind's eye I saw her parents and I knew, *they never had her back.* Forever after she would live her life trusting that no one would ever care for her. And as she spoke, and the recognition of these intense emotions attached to the linen closet surfaced, I saw them release, like black smoke, leaving the field of my client.

I held my breath. *Keep going,* my heart begged this woman. This beautiful soul had come to my office that day, searching for release from many physical issues—chronic hip issues, and lung issues, for which she received a protein fusion each week to support her lung function—issues she would need to endure for the rest of her life. Yet the guides in the room told me differently. I heard them say, *No.* As she spoke of other health issues, I heard the guides say, *No.* I knew this meant she would heal very soon, and she would heal with nature. She would heal the land, the plants, the trees. She would heal the animals. Her connection with the earth was strong. Immediately I felt guided to make her stand—it was time, the guides told me, that she be rewarded for her suffering.

She stood. Instantly I sensed the animals, the guides and the room full of spirits wanting to do the work. It was if they were fighting over her. I surrendered my hands and body to the guides. And I waited.

I saw her first chakra release—as it did, I felt the pull from my own root area. I knew this was hers, not mine. It was her rage, a fierce anger that sat deep in her groin area, sitting and stewing with the intention of causing disease. I could feel knives being removed or used in her second chakra. Her sacral chakra was traumatized by the abuse, and scar tissue was filling her. At that moment I wished I could hug her with all my might. I felt the guides restore and release the tissue, and a flood of healing light filled her with orange sparkling intensity. The Native Americans were clearing her first and second chakra, and I found that Joan of Arc, a warrior energy, came to light the fire in her solar plexus, right above her belly. Her will, her drive to survive had been burned out. Her life force was diminishing, and her third chakra was dark.

Don't be nervous, I told her in my mind, as I felt the fire ignite and swell up her spine, over her head and down the front of her body. The orbit of energy, the will returned to her. It was her heart that was so broken. Pieces were spread everywhere. I saw her, with the energy of the Mother Mary, picking them up, one by one, and carefully piecing them back together. I felt the energy flow, from my heart to hers. I was guided to open my heart. As the guide filled me, I was to fill her; it was for her, not for me. I was a servant to Spirit. The guides moved to the fifth chakra; it also was dark and stagnant. Screams had been pushed back, warned not to make a sound; this blocked her throat chakra from screaming the truth. With that, the silent screams poured out like dense smog, toxic pollution that had filled her grieving throat and lungs for so many years. With that, I saw the blue crystal light fill her. It was as though a poison had been locked in her body since childhood, and now that poison had been released.

Our eyes locked again, and she squeezed my hand. She'd come to me, trusting in me, wanting to believe in *something*. She'd become a mother and a wife, and had lived a good life despite the illnesses and negativity. Deep inside, she knew she had the ability to see, to feel, to know. Suddenly her sixth chakra blasted open and filled with violet light, and with that I felt the vibration come to the crown. The healing Light of clarity and her true self came pouring into the room. It had been waiting for so long to download, and it continued to expand, to flow, to pour out. She glowed with the inner Light—with rejuvenating Light, with the Light of gratitude, with the Light of clarity, and with the ability to heal.

We finished. Exhausted, she rose to exit, a different person. She will no longer be the person she was, I realized, the wounded spirit, the lost soul. Before leaving, she expressed to me that she connected to animals, believing she had the ability to relieve their pain—yet she had never told anyone. She revealed that while she was in the hospital crib as a young child, she spied a black puma cat sleeping next to her at all times. It circled her in her darkest hours. Now, for the first time since she was a child, she saw the black puma in my office. I understood: The puma felt her fear and anxiety. Just as it had all those years before, it made itself known, and she allowed herself to see and feel its loving protection. In the silence of her healing, she had spoken to her puma, told him that he should lay down, because everything was okay. She was going to be okay.

Our healing session gave her purpose; she entered my office a broken woman, and left remade in love, able to nurture her own soul. No longer would she sit in the pain of the past. Now she had work to be done, work she had put aside, work she had unknowingly ached and yearned for her whole life.

We both changed that day. Fearlessly, she became aware of her presence in this world as a servant, with a job to bring the Light. After her session, I also received clarity: I would no longer be defined by my own suffering, my own pain. I would live free, fully transformed. I would live life from the heart and speak my truth, and I would live my truths. I would live without judgment or shame in my gifts. I would live life seeing and accepting all the connections and guidance from Spirit. I would live accepting the Light and sharing its infinite restorative power. That day, I became who I was intended to be. An obedient servant of the Light, and a warrior of healing, putting Light in the hands of those who may be hurting.

As my story ends, my mind flashes back to 1988, and that dark highway that once swallowed up my future. Illuminated on the road ahead I now see Tom—18 years old, miraculously healed, his surfer muscles firm and his legs renewed, walking bravely into the bright hour of a new day.

This is what each of us must do.

We lift our eyes to the horizon. Place one brave foot forward, then another, following the Light on the road ahead. We march our bold hearts toward the dawning sunshine, the promise of the Light—with love, with trust, in a passionate search for our own truth. So long as the Light keeps shining on us, we march. We hope. We press. We struggle. We grow. We journey.

We *live*.